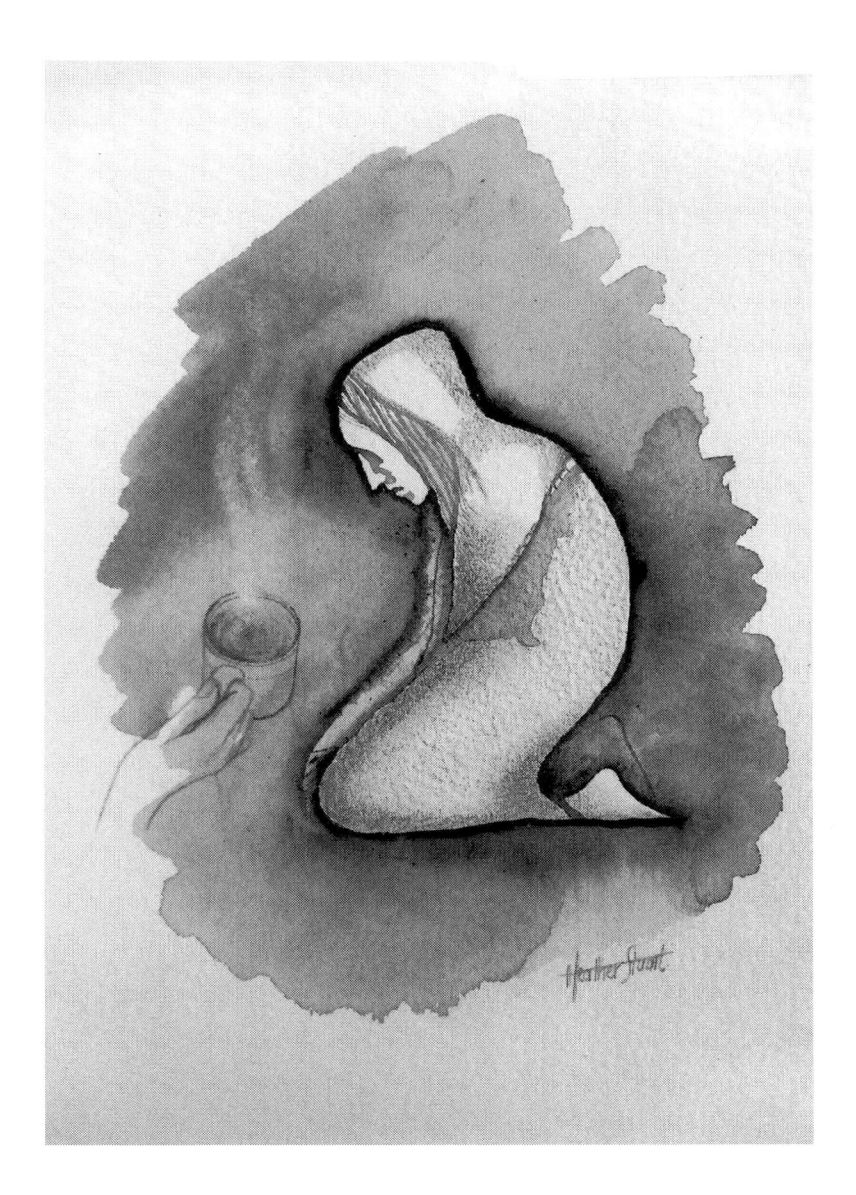

I need help

Published by Bourne to Write

Copyright © 2023 Matthew 25 Mission, Eastbourne

All rights reserved.

ISBN: 9798861243230

All proceeds from this publication go to Matthew 25 Mission.

Front cover: The Good Listener by Catriona Millar

catrionamillar.com

Voices from the Margins

Matthew 25 Mission, Eastbourne

Voices from the Margins

CONTENTS

	Acknowledgments	i
1	Introduction	Pg 3
2	The Nature of Matthew 25 Mission	Pg 8
3	Dark Places	Pg 12
4	Institutional Madness	Pg 28
5	Photographs	Pg 36
6	Attitudes	Pg 55
7	Lighter Moments	Pg 59
8	Who Am I?	Pg 68
9	Volunteer Perspectives	Pg 96
10	Mathew 25 Mission Prayer	Pg 101

This book is dedicated to the many in Eastbourne who honour us with their trust and friendship as they frequent the drop-in centre or browse in the charity shop. The stories of our guests need to be heard in these times and their concerns listened to and addressed.

We also dedicate this book to the many in Eastbourne who have volunteered in the past, and still do today in various ways in our M25M community. Whether cooking food, serving food and drink to guests, chatting with guests, working in the garden, serving in the shop, driving the van, communicating with our supporters, donating clothes and other goods, all are appreciated.

Although the Mission operates mainly on volunteers, this could not happen without the continued, consistent example and guidance of our Charity Manager, Chaplain, Key Workers and Board of Trustees, not forgetting all those who support us with their encouragement, prayers and finances month by month.

Introduction

Voices from the Margins evolved from a writing residency that Paul Howard undertook with Matthew 25 Mission as part of his MA in Creative Writing at the University of Brighton. The purpose of the placement was to seek inspiration for his own writing and to encourage others to share their stories in written or oral form.

From the outset, Paul's hope was that we would accumulate sufficient material to produce a book, the sale of which would benefit the charity. Whereas the formal course requirement was for a placement of about eight weeks, the ambition to publish an anthology resulted in the residency continuing for several months.

When Paul was not able to complete the work needed for the book, due to other responsibilities, Lesley Dawson took over collecting material from guests and added a section on the experiences of the many M25M volunteers. The motivations for volunteering at "the Mission" are many and varied. Some volunteers see what they do as an outworking of their Christian faith, as something that Jesus would have done, inspired by the parable in the 25th chapter of Matthew's gospel. Others have humanitarian motives for doing the same work, such as concern for their fellow man, and for some volunteering is a response to the help they and their families have received from the Mission and see this work as a way of giving back to the community.

The special quality of Matthew 25 Mission is probably best summed up in *'**The Pit of Poo**'*, which highlights the charity's drive to work alongside its 'guests' in whatever sticky and dark place they find themselves. Here, the fact that the organisation refers to the people it supports as 'guests' is deliberate and meaningful.

Moreover, it doesn't distinguish between those being supported and anyone else that sets foot in its Tardis-like premises, Brodie Hall, which stands next to Christ Church in Seaside, Eastbourne. All are welcome, the only condition of that openness being an acceptance of basic, unwritten rules of mutual respect. Even a person's known atheism is no barrier to inclusion in the Mission or this project. The guiding principles of this Christian charity would be equally at home in socialist circles and from the Mission's point of view, this project, with its emphasis on giving voices to people who frequently go unheard, was regarded as having its heart in the right place.

Homelessness and the many other reasons why the guests at Matthew 25 are marginalised, often take them where the challenges facing them are compounded and amplified. The harrowing first-hand accounts of these 'Dark Places' contain language that some readers might find offensive. If that is the case, we hope those readers will find it in their hearts to understand that such language is invariably born of the desperate plight and frustration of the authors of some of the pieces and not of a determination to shock and upset.

Although many people empathise with those in direst need in our society, it is a matter of great disappointment that many others do not. In our experience, during the last three or four decades our society has become increasingly shaped by selfishness, so much so that individual greed seems to be viewed as a virtue in some quarters. One consequence of the culture of 'looking after number one' is a decline in care for others. It is all too easy to see the people *with* a problem *as* the problem. As the pieces on '***Attitudes***' reveal, expressions of anger and disgust towards the marginalised are unfair, but they may help us avoid any responsibility for the conditions that created the marginalisation in the first place. In this section, the micro-fiction, 'The Bad Samaritan', illustrates the problem of aid with strings attached, an issue at a local level as much as it is on the international stage.

A recurring theme in the accounts of people on the margins of society is that the very agencies, which are purportedly there to help them, often compound their difficulties. The section entitled *'Institutionalised Madness'* throws a light on many of the encounters that homeless people have with officialdom. Often these experiences have a Kafkaesque quality.

For all the challenges they face and manage (in a way that many of us would fail to), many of the voices from the margins are laced with humour and wit, examples of which are gathered in the *'Light Moments'* selection.

That part of the anthology, entitled *'Who I Am'*, goes beyond the superficial labelling of someone as 'homeless' or 'addicted' to convey the diverse qualities of the guests at Matthew 25 Mission, an antidote to the negative attitudes described in an earlier section. Perhaps the thing that has stood out most of all is the mutual respect and support that marginalised people invariably show towards each other, behaviour that reminds us of George Eliot's observation on the human condition.

'What do we live for, if not to make life less difficult for each other?'

M25M would not be what it is without the staff and volunteers. Apart from the Manager, the Chaplain, the two Key Workers, a Kitchen Manager and a part time bookkeeper, all the rest of the over 50 people who help in various ways are volunteers. For this reason, it is appropriate to include their perspectives and explain how everything began.

How it all began

Brian Martin, the founder and first manager of the drop- in centre for vulnerable people in Eastbourne died in hospital just after Christmas 2020.

The charity was started in 1992, originally called Oasis Christian Outreach Trust, but changed its name to The Matthew Twenty-Five Mission in 2011. Initially located at the Elim Community Church on Upperton Road, the centre moved first to the Royal Hotel, Marine Parade and then to Brodie Hall at Christ Church on Seaside.

Brian was known for his practical Christianity and his ready smile. He persuaded many Eastbournites to support the centre by volunteering, giving of their goods and money and prayer.

He always gave people second, third and many other chances to sort out their lives and was never downhearted when they came back time after time and had to start all over again. Brian was not a well man, having had heart problems and cardiac surgery, he eventually handed the baton to Peter Thorley in 2008, who later handed over the Manager's job to Oscar Plumley and took on the role of Chaplain. Despite not being able to be as active as previously Brian would pop in to see us at Brodie Hall from time to time and send us generous cheques.

He had a heart particularly for those who were rough sleepers and sofa surfers and when he died, they lost a good friend and champion. Those of us who remember him do so with much love and great respect.

The Gospel of Matthew Chapter 25 verses 31 to 46

When the Son of Man comes in His glory and all the angels with Him, He will sit on His throne in heavenly glory.

All the nations will be gathered before Him, and He will separate the people one from another as a shepherd separates the sheep from the goats.

He will put the sheep on His right and the goats on His left.

Then the King will say to those on His right "Come, you who are blessed by my Father, take your inheritance, the kingdom prepared for you since the creation of the world.

For I was hungry, and you gave me something to eat, I was thirsty, and you gave me something to drink, I was a stranger and you invited me in.

I needed clothes and you clothed me, I was sick and you looked after me, I was in prison, and you came to visit me."

Then the righteous will answer Him "Lord, when did we see you hungry and feed you, or thirsty and gave you something to drink?

When did we see you a stranger and invite you in, or needing clothes and clothe you?

When did we see you sick or in prison and go to visit you?"

The King will reply "I tell you the truth, ***whatever you did for one of the least of these brothers of mine, you did for me."***

Then He will say to those on His left "Depart from me you who are cursed Into the eternal fire prepared for the devil and His angels.

For I was hungry, and you gave me nothing to eat. I was thirsty and you gave me nothing to drink.

I was a stranger, and you did not invite me in. I needed clothes and you did not clothe me, I was sick and in prison and you did not look after me."

They also will answer "Lord, when did we see you hungry or thirsty or a stranger or needing clothes or sick or in prison and did not help you?"

He will ***reply "I tell you the truth, whatever you did not do for one of the least of these, you did not do for me."***

Then they will go away to eternal punishment, but the righteous to eternal life.

The above quotation is the reason for the Matthew 25 Mission's existence.

The Nature of Matthew 25 Mission

The Pit of Poo

When asked to explain the values and principles of Matthew 25, Peter, our Chaplain tells this tale:

Someone is standing up to their knees in a large pit of poo, which is thirty feet across and surrounded by a bank. A crowd has formed on the bank and its members are hurling abuse and sarcasm at the stranded soul below.

We at Matthew 25 don't reach down and offer the person a hand with a view to pulling them out of the mire. We climb into the pit and stand by their side. We reassure them that, at some stage in their lives, nearly everyone ends up in the pit. And that we will remain with them until they're able to progress.

The person's problems don't end when they are able to climb out of the pit. For one thing, most people don't want to touch them as they carry the stench of where they've been. We remain alongside, helping them find the sources of ongoing assistance and supporting them in the process.

Then, we return to the pit and await our next guest, for it is important, when someone finds themselves in the pit of poo, that there is someone there to greet them without judgment.

Commandments

In my experience, most places that help the poor and homeless have a raft of rules to follow. Fair enough, I guess. When I first came across Matthew 25 Mission, I assumed that, as a Christian charity, it would be the Ten Commandments and all that.

As it turned out, they don't ram religion down your throat. They don't even ask if you have a religion.

For them the only issue seems to be that you have needs.

Of course, there *are* golden rules. Yeah, you've guessed, ten of them. And they're a lot harder to stick to than the list given to Moses back in the day. I've never coveted my neighbour's ox or knowingly made a graven image, and except for the occasional wasp, or fly, I've never killed. All pretty straightforward… unlike the ones posted on the wall of Brodie Hall.

- Laugh outloud
- Dream big
- Love always
- Be grateful
- Worry less
- Make memories
- Wake up smiling
- Stay positive
- Cherish every day
- Have fun

When I first saw the poster, I nearly choked on my full English breakfast. How was I supposed to achieve any of those, let alone all of them, while living rough? The funny thing is that these statements, more reminders of humanity than commandments, make a difference if you let them. Rather than seeing them as impossible goals, I started to adapt them to my circumstances. OK, so what if my big dream is to be alive tomorrow and there are days when I struggle to find something to be grateful for? The golden 'rules' are reference points, steppingstones which we can all make use of in the way that makes most sense to us. They don't magically make my hardships disappear, but they give me something to hold onto.

I'm Tired of Words

Over the years I've heard so many of them, promises given, suggestions made, and forms filled in, all of which have come to nothing. I wrote these words after leaving the latest church service where I was made much of and then allowed to walk out into the dark night alone. They all knew I was homeless, but nobody offered me even a sleeping bag or a flask of coffee to take with me.

If I hear one more Christian say, "may God bless you," or one more humanist telling me, "it's a tragedy that Eastbourne has no accommodation for homeless people. We are doing all we can to persuade the Council to change its policy," I shall scream. Despite all these promises of support I am still sleeping in a shelter on the seafront.

Life wasn't always like this. Once upon a time, many years ago, I was like all the other 'normal' people in Eastbourne. I was part of a happy family, mum, dad and me. We laughed a lot and had fun together. Then tragedy struck and my wonderful dad was killed in a fight outside our local pub. After that everything changed. My mum found she couldn't cope without him and began to take too many sleeping pills and tranquilisers. She took up with this nauseating man she met at a support group and, before you could say 'Jack Robinson', I had a new dad; except he wasn't my dad.

It was obvious that he didn't really want me around. He wanted mum all to himself; except when he tried to climb into my bed. I suggested that he had lost his way and come into my room by mistake. At this he smiled without it reaching his eyes and mumbled something about keeping it our secret and not telling mum. There was only so much of this I could take and, as soon as I could, I left home, staying at first with my best school friend. This was OK until her mum was sectioned and put into a secure unit and my friend went to live with her aunt up North.

After that I shacked up with various boys I had met at the Job Centre, but finally no-one would have us in their house.

I think this had something to do with me stealing from any purse I could find.

This morning on waking I wandered into town hoping to beg money from gullible people shopping in the new Beacon Centre. This older woman went past me, then backtracked and I thought, "Great, here comes another sucker". She grinned at me and, instead of putting her hand in her pocket, offered to buy me a coffee and burger at MacDonald's. I explained that I was banned from MacDonald's, so she brought the food and drink out to me. As she was leaving, she said, "Have you been to the Matthew 25 Mission? You can get food there all day."

"Here it comes," I thought, "I will have to go to a religious meeting before I get anything to eat" and prepared to swear at her to make her go away. However, she didn't say another word, just gave me a card with an address down Seaside. My feelings about Missions were so strong that it was three nights later when putting my hands in my pockets to keep warm that I found the card.

Next morning my stomach was so empty that I decided to chance going to the place. After all, I had become very good at tuning out sermons. I found the place and walked into this small building in front of the church, attracted by the tantalising smell of frying bacon. Now that was a breakfast. And believe it or not, nobody said anything to me after asking if I wanted breakfast. I sat there all day, drinking endless cups of coffee and nobody tried to chase me out or convert me.

I think I might go again.

Dark Places

Darkness is Cheap

Darkness is a place to hide away, where nobody can see you.
You can take what you want freely and there is no one to ask for payment.
Shopping in the dark is much cheaper with nothing to pay,
But not as much fun as buying in company with neighbours.

Visits in the dark are unexpected, visits in the dark are frightening.
Darkness is a place of shadows, of ghosts, of bogeymen, of prowlers, of thieves,
Predators sneak up on sleeping families in the dark
Children who cannot sleep without waking in fear.

I cannot see clearly in the dark
I need to be able to see what is coming so I can prepare myself for how to react.
You can creep up on me in the dark, you can hurt me in the shadows.
You can play on my insecurities in the dark, you can make me feel not in control.

Darkness is often linked with evil doings, bad things, wicked people.
Perhaps, instead it can be a way of hiding imperfections, of covering up blemishes,
Of shadowed colours and flattened shapes
Of smoothing out discrepancies, of beautifying common things.

Grieving/Surviving

I am a survivor of my son's suicide, but only just ...
I never thought that would be part of my identity, but if I must now wear this then ...
I choose to do it honestly and without shame.
I choose to wear my heart upon my sleeve in all its brokenness.
I choose to be a truth-teller, even if some days I have only the strength to speak in a whisper.
I choose to let tears fall and say the word 'suicide'.
I choose not to let the word 'suicide' haunt me and send me to grieve in isolation.
I choose to give meaning to my son's death.
Does that make me brave? I don't think so, but whatever it makes me I will do it with courage.
My love for my son was unconditional and forever.
So, when he chose suicide, he took the life out of me, the person who brought him into this world and into the family.
Do I feel angry? Do I feel guilty, sad, tearful, bewildered? Yes, all these feelings haunt me.
Everything has changed, my life, my whole existence, my relationships with others.
I am not the same person anymore.
I am a stranger.
My grief walks with me wherever I go, it wakes with me in the morning, it sits with me when I am eating, it walks with me in the rain and the sunshine, it sits on my shoulder when I shower, it stays with me when I go to bed. My grief is with me for the rest of my life.
It can be very difficult to recover from the death of a loved one, but it is more difficult if the individual took their own life.
The act of suicide left me with feelings of shame and guilt that I could have, should have, ought to have, done something to help stop this from happening.

People wonder how I can still stand, walk, even laugh occasionally … but they don't ask.

I am lost as I search for my son. I look to the sky each day and ask, 'Where are you, my son?', knowing he is not here. Instinct is to protect your children; I feel I have failed to protect my son.

The pain inside is debilitating, horrible, unremitting; it's impossible to think straight.

Normal everyday activities, getting up in the morning, eating, listening to others, jobs that need to be done, going to work, are hard to follow through. My mind wanders and it is hazy and out of focus, it feels full of cotton wool.

My tears are always on the cusp.

I try to carry on as if nothing has changed but everything has changed.

There is no fix or solution to my heartache, no going back in time for as long as I breathe.

I will never get over my son's suicide, but I try to get through it. I try to find a new normal, but what is normal now? There is a before, now there is an after.

Grief does not become smaller or disappear over time, grief stays the same, but life is supposed to grow around it. Other things in our life happen, but grief stays within us and at certain times, like birthdays, anniversaries, Christmas, you dip straight back into it.

I loved my son with a passion and always will.

I will say his name and speak about him as normally and naturally as non-bereaved parents do.

I may not make any more memories with him, but I will play the ones we had in my mind forever. And as each year passes, I will think about what my son would be doing now. How would he look as he aged? Grief lasts forever, the love I have for my son will last forever.

There is and always will be an empty chair, an empty space by my side. The empty space of my son.

He is a photo in a picture frame that I adore.

I miss my son … and always will.

Family

Family can be a blessing, or it can be a curse.
Family can bring happiness, or it can bring sorrow.
Family can help you in your darkest times,
Or leave you stranded in the uncertainty of the abyss.
Family can do a lot, they can help, or they don't.
They can be your hero or your nemesis.
But family will always be your biggest weakness, no matter what,
Good or bad.

The Broken Fantasy

Love is a demon in disguise,
Makes you do crazy things,
Controls you, takes over your mind.
Love is death itself.
Love hurts.
It breaks you in ways you never thought it could.
Love comes in all different forms,
So, it can destroy you in every way.
Love destroys you - it destroys your heart.

Hollow

He was alone in this world, with nothing but a broken heart and a damaged mind. No-one understood him, only his demons did.
He was in the dark, without a light to guide him to paradise. With nothing, with no-one, he was alone and neither God nor the Devil could save him.
His soul was decaying, no use to anyone. The voices in his head were growing louder, taking over his mind.
He felt better off going with the tall dark man on the horse, but the man upstairs wouldn't admit him, because he wasn't pure, and the man downstairs wouldn't take him because he had no soul to trade.
Of course, he could go where the monsters go, but that would be worse than living. So, he remained stuck, nowhere to go, no-one to go to.
Day in, day out, tortured by living in this big, bad world, he made it rain with his blood, creating a food of dark red misery.
His scars got deeper.
His darkness grew blacker.
The pain grew more intense.
He felt that he could not be saved, could not be loved, could not be happy.
No happy ending for him, however hard he tried.

Once an Addict, Always an Addict

A quick escape from this world, a way to forget everything and everyone.
Pumping through her veins like water in a swollen stream. One hit and it all goes away. One more mark and the pain goes.
The magical white rabbit helps her get through the day.

One more time, just one more hit, a quick high makes the world seem better. She doesn't care if she's messing up her body, for a bit of happiness in a tube in her eyes.

Her skin is decaying, her teeth are yellow, and her nails gone, but she doesn't care because she is free and fearless … so she thinks.

She may be broken but she still puts it in her veins. She is homeless, but she keeps inhaling it like sherbet.

She is selling everything (and I mean *everything*) so she can continue to fill her lungs with magical goodness, as she calls it.

She is the girl that no-one wants to become, the one you stay away from. She could've done so much better, but she fell hard, because everyone around her said to take the sugar pills and 'all your worries will disappear, all your suffering will just go, you will be free'.

What a beautiful lie. If only she had known the truth, then.

The Lonely Nights

The blade slices across her wrist like butter, the blood coming out like a waterfall. Tears falling down her face. Trying to hold it together. Seeing the blue veins makes it all too real.

The once shiny razor now a dark, thick red.

At first, she is scared but is coming to terms with this being the end and she's overcome with joy and happiness.

Her hands shake, the blood slows down, while her heart speeds up with the adrenaline coursing through her veins and whole being. She's falling in and out of sleep, a pool of blood surrounds her soon to be lifeless body.

Warmth leaves her body, leaving her ice cold.

Most would be terrified, not knowing what's next, but not her. She is happy to be leaving this world.

Poisoned Bliss

She takes pills to get through the day.
She hides behind a smile, laughs the loudest so no-one will hear her crying.
God knows she is trying, but Lucifer senses that she is giving up, day by day.
She's running through the darkness to find the light.
God knows she's trying, but Lucifer she's tiring of the fight.
Her hands ache from holding on, her eyes are empty.
Her heart is bleeding from the eternal sorrow.
From her head to her feet, she is soaked in dark, red syrup.
She is nothing and will forever be nothing.
When she goes down, no-one will be there.
She is unwanted, even the bugs won't touch her.
She will always be a lost soul, blessed by the angels and corrupted by the demons.

The Knight of the Shadows

People say he's a monster, I call him my hero.
He has many names, but to me he is Solution.
I dream about him when I visit Wonderland.
He is all I can think about, day and night.
When he is near, it takes my breath away.
I can't wait for the day when we'll be together, walking side by side into paradise.
He is everything to me and, sooner rather than later, we will be together.

Doll's House

Mummy and Daddy fighting over everything and anything are destroying their family.
Mama always working, never seeing her children.
Papa falling into the arms of darkness, not seeing what he's got.
The children always picking up the pieces and, while doing so, losing a piece of themselves every day.
Lost, damaged, a once happy family now a decaying mess of despair.
Mother only happy when she is with Jack Daniels.
Father only pleased when he's in control of everything and everybody.
The children are away with the fairies, the one happy place, their only escape from the chaos.
Once upon a time they were a happy family … or were they? Maybe they made themselves believe they were happy, so they could be like everyone else, but they just fell apart.

Suicide Note

Someone, anyone, could've saved him. He was afraid, alone, all he wanted was love. His mind was an ongoing war, keeping him awake. The voices were decaying his mind. No-one knew what was going on inside his head. Even he didn't know.
Someone, anyone, could've looked in his eyes and seen that he was breaking. His loneliness was killing him. He had no-one. He wanted someone, someone to save him. He wanted anyone to grab him tight and say 'Everything will be OK. I've got you'. The deeper his pain, the deeper the cuts. The pills were getting him by, but for how long could he keep going?

People say they understand but how can they if he doesn't? You could've saved him but it's too late, he was too far gone. His pain was never ending, the scars covered his body. The loneliness made him shut down.
The only thing he had was the darkness,
the darkness that held him while he cried himself to sleep,
kept him company while he swallowed the pills,
was all he had, the only thing by his side,
alone understood him,
was always there for him,
loved him even though he was broken.
So how the hell was he supposed to let go of the only thing that was there for him, the only thing that loved him even when he was so unlovable?

Behind the Mask

Fake smile, fake laughs.
Numbing the pain with drugs and blades.
Hallucinating on the daily trip, the voices growing louder and louder.
She knows she'll be dead by 20.
Pill popping day and night.
Self-harming has become her other drug, like cocaine, always on the edge, awaiting the next hit.
Pushing everyone away, she's convinced that she can take the world on by herself.
She's dead wrong.
Suicide on her mind daily.
Never knowing whether she's coming or going.
Her mind is a fucking war zone.
Put a gun in her hand and she'll pull the trigger before you know it, to shut her mind up for good.

Men Suffer Too

Mind is a prison.
No control, no hold on reality.
Losing it every fucking day.
Barely holding on to reality.
People have got his back, but he feels completely alone in this world.
Tired of saying 'Goodbye'.
Tired of holding on.
Trying to be strong for everyone, but he's lost all meaning of the world.

A Normal Day?

A normal day, like every other day. Waking up to the sweet sound of my mum's singing, I spring out of bed. The sun is shining and it's everyone's favourite day, sports day. Putting on my school P.E. kit and new Puma trainers, I sprint downstairs. Greeted by my mum, handing me a bowl of Cheerios and a glass of milk, I head for the front room.

I stop, confused by the sight of a man sitting in my chair reading the paper.

"Hello?" My voice is higher than I intended.

He lifts his head and grins, exposing teeth that clearly haven't had contact with a toothbrush for a long time. He puts a finger to his lips and mimes 'Sshhh'.

I walk back to the kitchen, making the excuse that I want to eat in the garden.

As I sit, I notice the hairs on my arms are standing high. Deep in thought. Why is there a creepy man in my home? In my chair! I am snapped out of my thoughts by raised voices. I listen hard, not daring to breath in case I miss something. I catch snatches.

"It's time to tell her. She's a sweet girl, she'll understand that her mummy and daddy don't love each other, that I'll be her new daddy.'

The words sting my ears, my eyes are streaming, my body shaking.

What does he mean? I have a dad. I love him.

Then it hits me. I was told that dad was working away but now I stop to think. Even when he is home he may as well not be. They're getting a divorce and this creep is going to be my new dad.

I walk back inside, pick up my bag and leave the house slamming the door.

The realisation hits me that I've never walked to school by myself. With too many emotions to handle, I run, blocking out the surrounding sounds, blocking out the world.

As I arrive at school, I stop, wiping the sweat from my face with the back of my hand and, taking a deep breath, look around. Everything seems normal, the usual people in their usual places. Like I said, a normal day like every other day. Except I would soon learn that for me there was nothing normal about today, the day that would change my life forever.

Darkness

A dark house in a dark village. The only sound is the vibrating fridge in the kitchen. I lie awake, scared to make a sound in case he hears me. Any chance of sleeping has been stolen by the man who lies in the very next room.

1. Six *Months Earlier*

Friday, leaving school, I look for my mum at the gates as I do every day. She's not here, no-one's here. The walk to my house isn't long, but I am yet to do it without mum. I decide to wait. She will come for me. I don't have any way of telling the time.

It's dark, an indication that it's late. I decide to walk home.

I stand before the place where my house used to stand. It has been replaced by a mess, a tangled pile of charcoal and brick. My family is nowhere to be seen. Confused, lonely and scared, I fall in a heap on the ground.

I am unaware of where I am, but it smells familiar. Slowly, I open my sleepy eyes and look around. I see white lights. I smell chemicals. I turn my head from left to right. White walls. I realise that I am in a hospital bed. A woman comes over, a sad smile on her face. As she approaches, I get a nervous feeling buzzing through my body. The woman takes my hand in hers. As she begins to talk, I hear words, but nothing registers in my head. I'm crying but don't understand why.

I am in a daze, a daze that is cut short by the sound of footsteps growing louder. Two men stand towering over me, hats in their hands. I hear the words 'family', 'died' and 'tragic accident', everything else is a blur. I sit in silence a single tear rolls down my face. I am left alone. I drift into unconsciousness.

Woken by the sound of shouting, I quickly sit up, alarmed.

They are shouting my name. I am blinded by the flashes of cameras and deafened by the noise.

As I try to block out everything and everyone, I am suddenly aware that I am in hospital, but why? I don't feel unwell, I am not in pain, I'm not hooked up to any machines. I lean forward to retrieve the notes that are normally at the end of the bed. There's nothing. Why am I here? It then occurs to me that I'm the only one on the ward.

2.

It's been twenty-seven days, sixteen hours, and four minutes since I woke up in hospital, unaware of how my life would be turned upside down. Let me tell you what's happened during those twenty-eight days. I woke up in hospital to be told that my entire family had been burnt to a crisp along with the building I once called home. I was found at the scene and since then I have been stuck in this hospital, a hospital for the mentally ill.

I have been questioned and suspected of murdering my family. The drugs they are forcing down my throat are clouding my memory. Did I kill them?

It's 3.15 p.m., time for group counselling. The same people, the same time every day. I am struggling to remember a time before these four walls, a time before I was a suspected murderer. I've learned a lot about myself that I didn't know before … or did I? I was an innocent, chubby ten-year-old without a care in the world. Now I am so skinny you can see every bone in my body, not a curve to be seen. My eyes, once glowing, are now as dull as a nearly burnt-out lightbulb. My hair is a knotted mess. My arms and legs are covered in scars; scars upon scars; each week a new set of scars appears. "Find a way to replace the silent pain," they said. "It will help you heal." My neck is bruised from the noose I made from bed sheets. This is me, unrecognisable.

3.

For one hundred and twenty-seven days I've been held against my will in this hospital. The same routine, day in day out, punctuated by visits from the police. The autopsy came back. My parents and siblings were burnt alive. The fire was started by the front door, but all evidence was destroyed. The charges have been dropped. I didn't kill my family, but they are still investigating.

It's Friday, time for my fortnightly visit. I get taken through to the same room as usual, seeing the same man I always see. Uncle Tom, that's what he calls himself, as do all the staff. I'm sure I didn't know him before I came here, but he knows me. He can tell things about me that I thought only my parents would know. Why haven't I told anyone that he's not really my uncle? He brings me sweets and talks to me like he really cares what I've got to say. He knows my family, tells me my mum would want him to look after me. What reason do I have not to believe him? It's what my mum would have wanted, right?

4.

Today is the funeral. I have no idea what to expect. The only people from the outside world I've had communication with for the last five months are the police and Uncle Tom. I haven't been beyond the gates since the day I arrived. I stand in my room, dressed in a black dress and black shoes. I've never worn a dress in the eleven years I've been alive. I asked for black shirt and suit trousers, but Uncle Tom said little girls wear dresses. I refused to brush my hair so the staff would be forced to cut it; instead, they left me as I was.

I get in the car with three members of hospital staff, because I'm not trusted by myself. I'm sure the staff still think I did it. I've heard them talk.

We arrive, I'm not sure where exactly, but I know we're here. Cameras await, but for whom?

There are people with banners. What do they say? One of my guards taps my shoulder. Somebody opens the car door. Once again, I am blinded by flashes and deafened by shouting, which brings me back to that day in hospital, which seems a lifetime ago.

I am walked through the crowd to the church. I turn around and catch a glimpse of the banners. 'YOUNGEST CHILD MURDERS ENTIRE FAMILY AND WALKS FREE'. Free? I've been locked up since it happened, and the police dropped all charges. What do these people know that I don't?

I am escorted through a side entrance to the first pew at the front of the church. I sit alone, the staff having taken their seats at the back of the church. Silence fills the air. The church doors open and within seconds the whole place is flooded with people. I stay still, eyes peeled, staring at the wooden boxes that contain the remains of my beloved family. A sharp pinch is the last thing I remember.

5.

Opening my eyes, I try to lift my hand to wipe the sleep away. I can't move it. I can't move anything. I wait for my eyes to adjust to the darkness. I look around with my eyeballs, unable to move my head. My eyes are fuzzy. I can't see anything other than a flashing red light somewhere above my head. Where am I? I try to use my other senses, but I can't smell anything unusual, nor can I hear anything other than the thumping of my heart. There is no daylight, or is it that I am unable to see it? How long have I been here?

6.

It's impossible to say how long I've been here, as I've not seen daylight since the funeral. I've not seen anyone either. Food and water are always on the floor when I wake up. But who brings it?

I am yet to work out where I am. I am no longer chained down, just chained at my left ankle. I start to imagine what could have happened. Suddenly my eyes open wide, and my ears pin back; there are voices outside, low and hushed. I shimmy closer to the door, making as little sound as humanly possible. I hear a man's whispers but can't make out his words. I strain to lean forward and hear a woman's voice. All the hairs on my body stand to attention. It can't be, can it? I listen so hard it hurts my brain. I want to scream. I shake my head. It can't be, it's impossible, right? Mum?

7.

I've pushed it out of my mind. My mum is dead. My mind is playing tricks. What day is it? What month? What year? I stand up, my eyes permanently adjusted to the dark. Walking a little, mainly crawling; my muscles are weak. I hear no voices, only heavy breathing. It sounds like a worn- out dog, just the other side of the door. I scan the room and realise there's no food or water. I try to recall the last time I had something in my mouth. Realisation kicks in, along with the hunger pains and headaches. I touch myself. I was never overweight but now every bone is sticking out. I look down. Bruises. Have I been beaten? I feel my arms, small lumps around the crease. Whoever is holding me here, has been drugging me.

Institutional Madness

Housey, Housey

A good crowd in today, as usual. Same old faces and a few new ones. If only I'd set out earlier, I'd be further up the queue. Chatting while we slowly shuffle forward. Monochrome images of prisoners and internees from war zones come to mind.

"How's it going?"

"You know how it is, struggling to make my second million."

"Yeah, it's tough at the top."

"Not all bad news. I had a good breakfast before coming here."

"You lucky devil. How did you blag that?"

"All above board, place on Seaside, next to the church up from the TA Centre."

"How do you get in?"!

"Open the door."

"I mean …"

"Just turn up. They're great people, really care. Unlike this lot."

"Edward Wilkins."

I step forward for my first interview of the day. Previous experience tells me it won't be the last.

I receive a stony-faced greeting, of sorts. "Good morning, Mister Wilkins. What can we do for you today?"

I resist the temptation to give a stream of facetious answers. Trying to be smart doesn't get you far in this place.

"I'm looking for accommodation, same as last week."

"Date of birth?"

"Haven't you got it on file?"

"I need you to confirm it."

"Fourth of May, nineteen sixty-four."

"National Insurance number."

"What's in the top corner of that folder is correct."

A bemused look.

"I can read upside down."

"If you're trying to be clever …"

"I'm not. I'm keen to get on with this, find somewhere to live."

My adversary, sorry, the official who is kindly trying to address my misfortune, punches a few keys.

"Take a seat in Waiting Area 'D'."

"Thank you."

Why does officialdom assume that our time is less precious than anyone else's? I'm homeless, jobless, and penniless, but a life, any life, is a life and mine is as valuable as the next person. I find as comfortable a position as the shabby black stacking chair permits and take a paperback from my coat pocket. I'm prepared for a long wait. Dostoyevsky's 'Notes from the Underground.' Does that surprise you? I'm not illiterate. I'm interested in nineteenth century Russian literature. Yeah, I'm a bit of an intellectual on the q.t. *I am a sick man … I am an angry man. I am an unattractive man.* Unlike me!

In the time it takes the anonymous narrator to recount his confrontation with the military officer I have gone nowhere. It's so hot in here. Is it a deliberate policy to make the punters feel uncomfortable? If so, it's wasted energy. Every soul this side of the barrier is here because of unimaginable discomfort from the slings and arrows of life on the edge. My eyelids droop. I didn't sleep so well last night, or the night before, or any night in recent memory. I start to dream of a duel with antique pistols. Me against the Secretary of State for Work and Pensions, who is dressed as a Russian army officer. *Six paces. Turn. Aim.*

"Edward Wilkins. Edwards Wilkins. Last call for Edward Wilkins!"

Another check of my personal details, a replay of my housing and homelessness history, enquiry about changes in my circumstances.

"I'm a week older than when we last met and a tad more desperate."

"Circumstances unchanged?"

"Affirmative."

A moment of optimism. "I'll see what we've got for you. Take a seat in waiting Area 'C'."

Moving up the alphabet. Moving five paces to the right across the invisible border. Graduating from shabby black chairs to shabby red ones. A terrible omen? I was in the black, now I'm in the red.

Another hour in the company of Fyodor.

"Edward Wilkins."

Oh, it's *him*. A real whatsit. The ultimate jobsworth. Not a shred of empathy. And if you make the mistake of talking about your predicament? He hits back with how tough it is for *him*! Cuts. Decline in housing stock. Pay freeze. All in it together.

My heart bleeds.

I can tell he's got nothing for me before he opens his mouth. That's right, I can read faces as well as books.

"I don't think we've got anything today."

I don't plead, – I retain my dignity against the odds – I assert, 'I need somewhere to live, to get myself back on track, to start fulfilling my ambitions'.

Between you and me, my main ambition is to still be here tomorrow. Here, in the land of the living, not the Housing Office.

"Look around. You're not the only one. And do you suppose they give us the resources we need?"

What did I tell you? I switch off for the next three minutes as he goes through his 'poor me' routine.

I try a different tack, "I can see how difficult it is for you. I wouldn't want your job for all the tea in China."

Not a hint of irony. Okay, I confess, a little.

"Is there nothing you can do?"

"Go to Waiting Area 'B'. I can't promise, but …"

To the untrained ear that might sound promising.

Mine is trained. It's another fob-off, thinly veiled as compassion.

Green seats. A symbol of recovery.

As I predicted, this is the shortest wait.

I am summoned back to the checkpoint by a different officer.

"Sorry, Mister Wilson *(sic)*, nothing for you today."

Once more I find myself next to the guy with the proper breakfast. He must have had a similar experience.

"No joy?"

"No. You?"

"No."

"Going anywhere special?"

"Nah, just dinner at The Grand."

"Pity, I was going to take you to the place in Seaside for the evening meal."

"Sounds good. To be honest, I've grown bored by haut cuisine. I think I'll skip The Grand this once."

Citizen of Nowhere

I was born and grew up in Eastbourne, before moving in with my girlfriend in Hastings. We had a kid, a beautiful daughter, and life was sweet. But you can never take anything for granted. The wheels came off our relationship and I found myself on the streets.

Obviously, I wanted to keep in touch with my daughter and approached Hastings Housing Office. I didn't know what to expect.

"You're from Eastbourne."

"I've been living here for five years."

"You're from Eastbourne."

"I've got a three-year-old daughter here."

"You're from Eastbourne."

"You won't help me then?"

"I can't, you're …"
"… I know, I'm from Eastbourne."

Next day, Eastbourne Housing Office.
"Sorry, I can't help you."
"What?! Why?!"
"You've been living in Hastings."
"But I'm from Eastbourne."
"You've been living in Hastings."
"They said I had to come here, 'cause I'm from Eastbourne."
"You were, but you're not anymore."

I went to the library, studied a map and wondered whether there was a Housing Office at Norman's Bay!

Two Months of Living Hell

The landlord was genuinely sorry, "You've been a good tenant, but I've been hit with some very hefty bills and have no option but to sell up."

I wondered what sort of financial mess Georgios had got himself into. I came up with a shortlist of three: a failed property deal in his native Cyprus, HMRC catching up with him over a shedload of unpaid tax or being deep in debt with the organisers of an illicit card school.

'And the winner is … gambling!'
Pay up inside a month or you'll get a visit from Hefty Bill.
"How long have we got?"
"Two months."

I know my rights. After the recurring nightmare of homelessness, I've become an expert in these matters. I'm entitled to two months from receipt of official notice.

Georgios looked down at a pair of shoes. His or mine? I wasn't sure. It didn't matter. His gaze averted, he handed over the envelope, "Your official notice," he muttered.

"I'm really sorry, Jay."

"Don't worry, Georgios. I'm sure those nice people at the Housing Department will see me right."

Of course, I was sure of the complete opposite, but I saw no point in lumping more discomfort on him than he was already experiencing. It's not much fun, watching someone age from fifty to seventy in a matter of minutes. I placed a firm hand on his shoulder, simultaneously reassuring him and guiding him out of the flat.

I joined my seven-year-old son in the lounge. "What is it, Dad?"

"Nothing Jack."

"But I heard Mister Georgios talk about selling up and … official notice."

On occasions like this I want to be the protective father, keep Jack safe from the world's worries.

Who am I kidding? Jack has had almost as much nomadic experience as I have. He could produce his own, junior version of 'Homelessness for Dummies'.

I flopped onto the sofa next to him, wrapped an arm around him and pulled him close.

"Try not to worry, Jack. I'll start sorting this out in the morning."

Dave, the builder I work for, is very understanding. He lets me do flexible hours around Jack's schooling. I've never asked, but I think Dave has had a stint as a single parent. After a while, you get a sense of these unstated things. Whenever Jack spends time with his mum or grandparents, I make myself available and am prepared to put in mega shifts.

"Of course, Jay. Get down there as soon as you've dropped Jack off at school. I'm expecting heavy rain, so we'll probably not be on site for long tomorrow. Not that the weather makes any difference. You've got to get down to the Council, come what may."

I thanked him and told him I'd make it up to him.

"No need, mate. A dad's gotta do what a dad's gotta do."

It's hard to describe my feelings as I walked from the municipal car park to the Housing Office. There were so many contradictory emotions swilling about - anger, hope, resignation, and determination for starters – that 'cocktail' is probably the best description. Not for the first time, my life was in turmoil. At least my emotions were in step with my life.

When the going gets tough, I put a brave face on, mainly for Jack's benefit. I don't know why I do it because he can see through me. I guess it's something deep in the parental psyche. The drive to shield your kids. Something that comes naturally, that you can't suppress even if it's as useful as a chocolate teapot.

To be honest, I'm as convinced by the beaming optimism as Jack. Nevertheless, I sat my brave face down opposite my allotted housing adviser.

The good news was that, as a child was involved, I'd receive priority treatment.

The not so good was that I'd have to wait until we were evicted before the Council would act.

Surreal or what?

And there was I thinking I knew everything about the mysterious workings of the housing Gods.

"You mean to tell me that you'll only help us on the day we're out on our ears?"

"We've got no option."

"Ever heard of prevention being better than cure?"

"I'd like to help, but..."

"...Your hands are bound with red tape."

"You do have options."

"Really?"

"You don't have to comply with the eviction notice."

"Eureka! Why didn't I think of that? I refuse to budge, leaving my landlord no option than to call in the bailiffs, who'll bill him a packet for doing something they'd probably enjoy even if money wasn't involved. He'll then add the bailiff's fees to my rent.

The sale of the building will fall through, and he'll end up in the County Court or the canal. Meanwhile, I'll apply for you to pay my debt to the bailiffs, which you'll be obliged to do. And throughout this crazy process, my son will have nightmares, regress to his bed wetting days and, if the bailiffs get their timing right, will be there to witness all our stuff being carted out from the flat and dumped in the street."

"You must do what's best for your son."

I sat motionless.

My adviser couldn't hold my gaze for more than a few seconds at a time, but had to keep looking back, for fear I was about to vault across the table with a non-verbal response. (I have no history of violent behaviour, but he doesn't know that. In his shoes, I'd be more than a little wary.)

"How much?"

"I beg your pardon?"

"How much do I have to pay for your stunning advice to look out for my son's interests?"

"There's no char...."

His words followed me towards the exit, but I'd stolen a march. They'd not catch me up.

I stepped into the rain. Dave's forecast had been right and no doubt the others would soon be in a bar, drowning their insincere sorrows over a day off work. I turned the collar of my jacket up and ran to my car. Next stop, the newsagent for a local paper, then back home to start the search. As ever, my best hope of finding somewhere to live rested with yours truly.

Brodie Hall, Christ Church

Ready for a meeting

Lunchtime at the Centre

Cleaning the floor

Presentation materials

Running repairs

Voices from the Margins

Our resident artist

Welcoming guests to the Centre

The Music Group

All Packed And Ready To Go

Saying goodbye to Brian Martin

Working in the charity shop

Beautifying the building

Receiving an award

Voices from the Margins

A Choir That Supports Us

The Christmas Fair

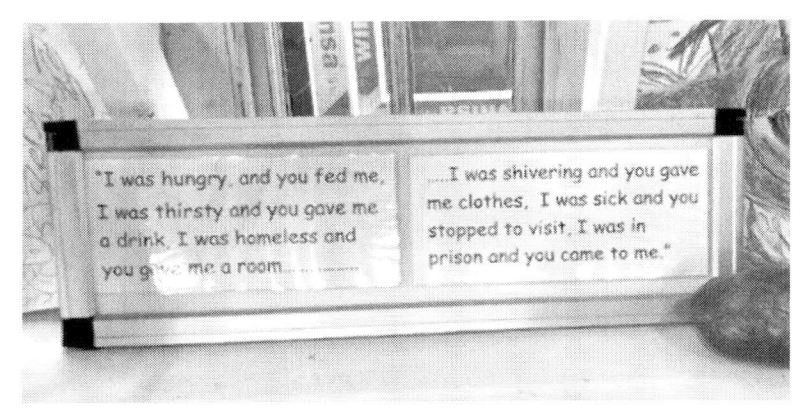

"I was hungry, and you fed me, I was thirsty and you gave me a drink, I was homeless and you gave me a room...... ....I was shivering and you gave me clothes, I was sick and you stopped to visit, I was in prison and you came to me."

The mission text

The shop that became our charity shop

Voices from the Margins

All too much!

Volunteers Lunch

Art exhibition

Voices from the Margins

The artist and his painting

Asking for help

Voices from the Margins

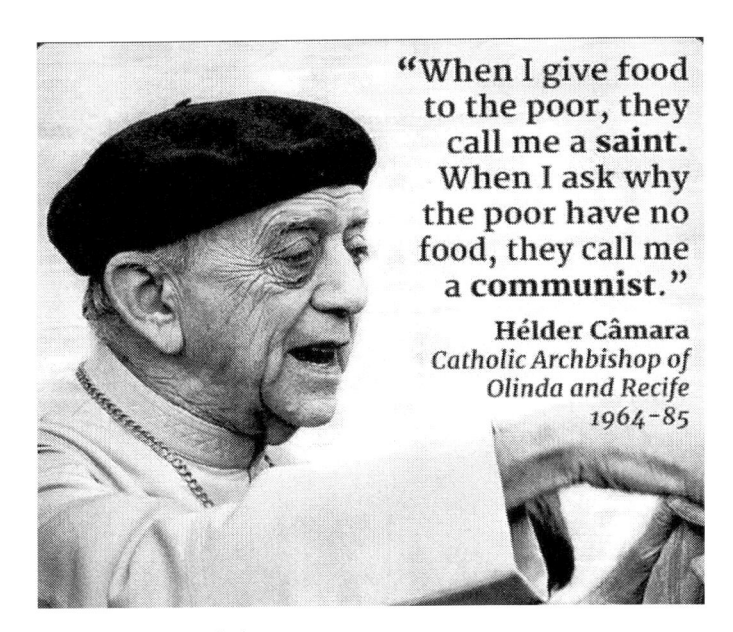

> "When I give food to the poor, they call me a **saint**. When I ask why the poor have no food, they call me a **communist**."
>
> Hélder Câmara
> *Catholic Archbishop of Olinda and Recife*
> *1964-85*

Saint or Communist?

Blaming or sharing

Too much paperwork

Sharing with my dog

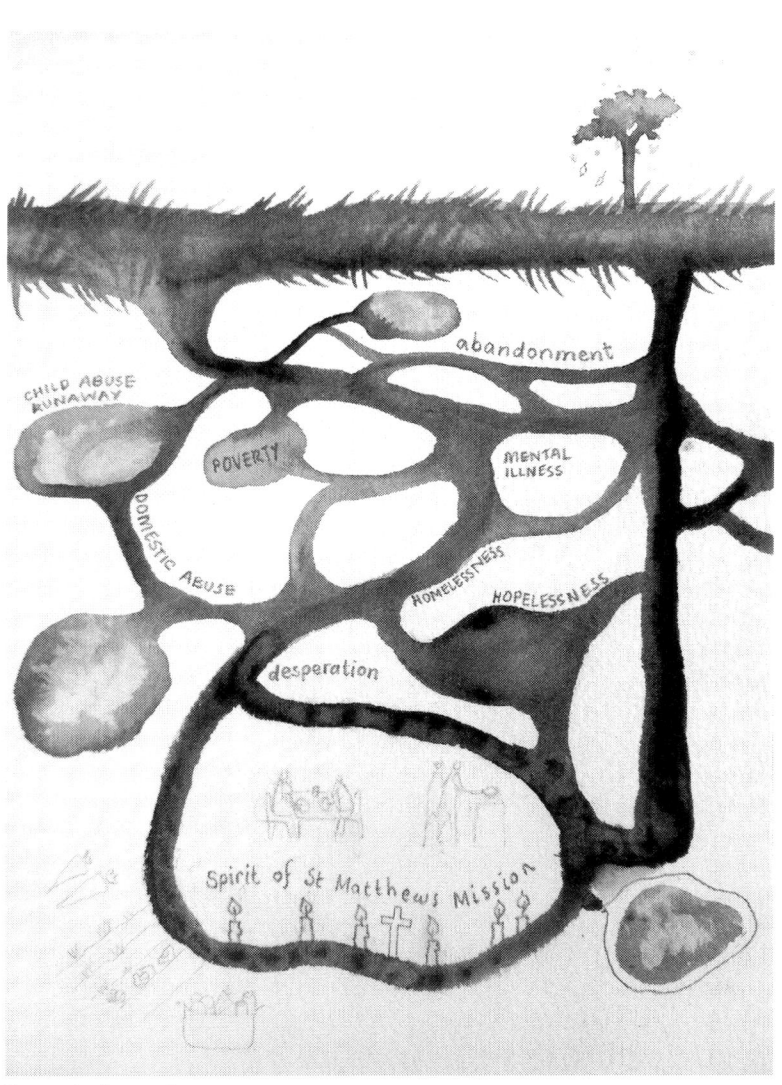

Beneath the surface

We need to stop just pulling people out of the river.

We need to go upstream and *find out why they're falling in.*

-Desmond Tutu

IT'S OK IF ALL YOU DID TODAY WAS SURVIVE.

Perhaps the butterfly is proof that you can go through a great deal of darkness and still become something beautiful.

Attitudes

You Heard

You heard him,
The bigot in the Post Office queue,
Bemoaning the loss of his beautiful town,
Its heart ripped out by the invaders,
With their matted hair,
Sleeping bags and cardboard.
No wonder all the shops are closing.
Who wants to shop in the High Street,
When it means running the gauntlet
Of the scum and their dogs,
Cans, bottles and fag-ends?
You heard him,
And you said …
Nothing.
Does the name Niemöller ring a bell?

He is Drunk!

The man coming down the street towards us staggered from side to side and was in danger of falling flat on his face. As people saw him coming towards them, they deliberately crossed the other side of the street. As they did so, they looked down their noses at him and curled their lips. It was as if they could smell the alcohol on him just by association.

She wanted to do the same, especially after she saw his mud-stained clothes and his shaven head but found it was difficult to turn aside when her arm was held in a vice-like grip by her best friend.

"Please don't tell me you are going to speak to this man? He looks as though he might attack us."

"Of course, I am going to stop and to speak with him."

I recognized him as a man who had spent all day the previous Wednesday at the drop-in centre. I had been told he had just come out of rehab and had downed a bottle of vodka immediately after he hit town. Ah well, I thought, that rehab was wasted, wasn't it?

As the day went by, I learned more about Paul. Whenever he stood up and lurched towards the door to smoke a cigarette or staggered towards the toilets, he used the walls, furniture and people to help him along his way. At one point, he reached out his hand to me to ask for help in getting back to his seat and cup of coffee. Underestimating his weight and the effects of gravity, he almost had us both on the floor but fortunately, Jason, one of the key workers grabbed us both.

I began to look at him differently. My professional background reminded me of a young man I had treated years before who had developed something called peripheral neuropathy affecting the nerves in the spinal cord.

"Paul's problem is not just alcoholism, is it?"

"No, we think he has had a head injury at some point in the past. If you look at his scalp there is a long scar on the left-hand side."

I remember the day when both key workers were on the phone from 9.30am until 2.30pm trying to get Paul housed. I shivered as I thought of the temperature and weather the night before. I couldn't imagine what it must have been like sleeping rough in that.

Paul had been born and raised in the town, so the local council had a duty of care to find him accommodation. During the day he had been warm and fed but as the afternoon approached and went, the calls became more urgent.

I overheard some of the conversation with the Housing Department, from both sides as the phone was on loudspeaker.

"We have been asking that he be housed since early this morning. Surely by now someone has found something for him."

"We had to work out if he is eligible for emergency accommodation."

"But Adult Social Care agreed that he is a vulnerable adult, so he is eligible."

"I'm afraid that is another department, so I can't comment on what they have said."

"Don't you guys talk to each other?"

"I will need to speak to my supervisor and ring you back."

"How long will that be?"

"I can't tell, as the decision is not up to me."

At the end of the day, I heard Mary beginning to lose her cool.

"So, you just expect us to close up the centre and go off to our comfortable, warm homes and leave him on the street?"

There was no answer to this, and we had to turn Paul and a couple of others out into the cold, windy late afternoon. It wasn't until three days later that Paul was given a room in a council housing project. Seeing him today, I wanted to ask him how it was going there.

Hearing this story my best friend asked, "So where was the Good Samaritan in all this?"

This Used to be a Nice Town

A large hard-breathing, middle-aged, slow man, with a mouth like a fish, dull staring eyes and sandy hair standing straight upright on his head, looked as if he had just choked and had that moment just come to. He sat down on the bench at the required social distance away from her and gave her a nauseating, fiendish grin that she returned with a brief nod. She hoped he was not going to talk to her. She hated it when strangers spoke to her and this character was very strange.

Out of the corner of her eye, she observed him take a brown paper bag out of his packet and open the top. Heavens, she thought, what has he got in there? It became abundantly clear as he lifted the mouth of the bag to his mouth, and she saw a bottle inside the bag.

Oh no! Not an alki she thought, that is all I need. The man glugged from the bottle quickly and then coughed loudly.

"That's better" he said, "Nothing quite like a few slugs of vodka to make you wake up" and offered her a drink.

"No thank you. I don't approve of drinking in the street and anyway, isn't it against the law?" His mouth opened wider and his eyes, though still dulled, gazed at her and then then around the area where they were sitting. He finally spoke "Well, I don't see a policeman around anywhere, do you? Go on missis, enjoy yourself for once. It will perk you up no end. You look as though you could do with a pick-me-up"

"No thank you" she said louder than she intended and began to gather her things together.

"Please don't go" he said plaintively "I don't have many people to talk to"

"I'm not really surprised, if you offer vodka to everyone you meet." She stood up and turned towards the pier. As she walked away, she said to herself, this used to be a nice town with respectable people living here. I don't know what has happened to it. I don't think I like it or the people you meet here now.

Lighter Moments

The Duel

Barry's a big guy, in physique and reputation. Whether or not all the stories about him, mainly told by Barry, are true, there's no doubting that he has presence. Or that he was hardened by his upbringing, by the company he once kept and by his recent difficulties. Barry's been in and out of temporary accommodation for years, interspersing crappy flats or rooms in equally crappy houses with sofa surfing and rough sleeping.

Despite his own problems, Barry never thinks twice about lending a helping hand to others. This, as much as the tales of his violent history, sets him up as the Godfather of the centre. More in the religious sense than the Mafia connotations, but, for all that, you don't mess with Barry. Fully aware of Barry's good works, the manager allows him to act important, so long as he remains within the centre's rules of mutual acceptance and respect.

This morning, as usual, he is at his preferred table, on his preferred chair, tucking into his full English, each mouthful chewed slowly and rolled around as if he was using the food to conduct a dental examination. During meals, he bows his head, focusing on a point a couple of inches beyond his plate, in complete contrast to his confident gaze when interacting with others.

The seat opposite Barry is empty. It has his best mate's name on it. Malc. He and Barry are almost inseparable. This dates from the time 'The Don' walked in on Malc getting a beating from a group of youths in a seafront shelter. He gave each of the attackers a little tap where no bruises would show but which would hurt like hell for an hour or so. Enough to teach them a lesson without causing serious injury.

Andy, a relative newcomer enters. One of the youngest of the guests, he is dressed in shabby chic; baggy joggers, a hoody two sizes too big for him and a faded bandana. Without pausing, he walks over to Barry's table and slithers into Malc's chair. The morning chatter ends as suddenly as a fly hitting a highspeed train. One of the volunteers takes a step towards them, but the manager halts his progress with a light touch on the forearm.

Barry pushes his plate to one side and gets to his feet. He and Andy stare each other down for a few moments. Barry clenches both fists and holds them a little way in front of him. Andy leans over and slaps Barry's right fist. He's got some bottle, or a death wish. Barry looks down at his right hand. "OK, son. You've got the first move."

Barry sits back down and pulls the chessboard to the centre of the table.

A Memorable Day

"I insist that I should be able to take that shot again."

"You can insist all you want. It won't get you anywhere."

"You can see I was distracted."

"Maintaining concentration is the personal responsibility of all competitors."

"It's unfair."

"It's the rules."

Thursday. I woke early. I woke early not because it was Thursday. I always wake early. How early? Sometime between three and three thirty. Always. I don't choose it. It's when my alarm clock goes off. Without fail. Let me explain. My alarm is an owl which roosts in one of the trees at the end of my 'garden'. Of course, it's not mine, other than in the sense of possession being nine tenths of the law. The other tenth will probably show up soon and ask me to move on. It's not a garden either, more a park, although it has a few flowerbeds. They look lovely from May onwards.

It's March, so their appearance is a bit forlorn.

The park has an odd lay-out. A large open space with a playground, putting course, tennis courts, and a smaller section, which appears tacked on as an afterthought by a planner who wasn't very good at planning. This smaller area has a bowling green, a refreshment kiosk, and a patch of grass around a covered bench. That's home, my current unfixed abode. Again, I need to qualify my ownership. Each day, I gather my bedding and possessions together, load them into the vehicle, which was donated by my sponsors, Marks & Spencer, which I then park as far out of sight as possible in the bushes behind the hut. It's a bit of a faff, but the routine serves a couple of very important purposes. First, it reduces the amount of attention I draw to myself. Second, it's only right that I free up the bench for other people to use. This is a public park and I care about stuff in common ownership.

I take up residence again before dusk, although I don't have sole use at nighttime. There's a family of foxes nearby and they make regular visits to see if I've been careless with my food storage. I've got the measure of them. Anything fresh goes in the two plastic boxes I've acquired on my travels. Everything else is in tins. But you know what they say about foxes; cunning and adaptable. I expect to wake up one morning to find they've attacked my provisions with a can opener.

The foxes aren't the only curious animals in the neighbourhood. The local dog walkers, who routinely use the park's larger plot, have taken to visiting this small section. My section. It's quite comical watching them use sign language to inform each other of my presence. As for their attempts at nonchalance as they saunter over having thrown their dog's balls near to the shelter, they're pure farce. No doubt one of them will grass me up to the council. Then, depending on how busy they are, a posse will appear with my marching orders in the following week.

I try not to be bitter about negative attitudes towards me, just wish these people would stop and think for a moment. A little tolerance and humility wouldn't go amiss.

'There but for the grace of God…' I may not add much to the aesthetic beauty of the park but at least I don't crap on the putting green.

They're not all bad – the people, not the dogs, which generally are friendly enough. One guy regularly checks in on me. He has what I call a bog-brush dog. Some sort of terrier. He occasionally brings me some food. Provides useful information, like where I can get my phone charged. Don't get me wrong. I appreciate his help. But I'm a bit wary of people who want to get too close. They tend to end up asking too many questions. Life's uncomfortable enough without someone prying.

Thursday is laundry day. The local facilities open at six and by six fifteen I've been to the loo, changed into fresh underwear and am busy cleaning my smalls in one of the basins. Life on the streets is a never-ending learning walk. There's no end to what I discover, like the effectiveness of the soap in the dispenser. Better than any detergent in my view. After a few minutes of rubbing and rinsing the water is coal black and my vest, pants and socks restored to respectability. To the dryer. The weather determines how long I hold my clothes under it. Today's sunny and breezy. A short burst of hot air to remove surface water, then I hang them up on a line that I erect between the hut and the kiosk. If I'm lucky, my clothes will still be there when I get back at the end of the day. Catch 22. If I don't wash them, they're not very nice to wear and I'm not very nice to be around, but, at least, no-one nicks them. Washed, they enhance my respectability and approachability and increase their attractiveness to 'thieves'. It's usually only kids having a laugh, but it isn't easy finding grey socks in a holly bush after dark.

With everything tidied away, I embark on my busy daily schedule, blissfully unaware that my drying underwear will lead to the least accurate shot ever seen on that green and prompt the only recorded instance of pushing, shoving and slapping in the history of bowls.

A Hold Up?

Her slight frame told of her inability to overpower a foe. Her kindly, wrinkled face offered the additional reassurance that, if she possessed the power, she wouldn't use it. She mounted the steps. She didn't know where to start. She used all of her inconsiderable weight to prise open the swing door. There was no manual on where to begin. She was the only person in the foyer. That removed some of the awkwardness that she'd anticipated and feared. She stepped forward to the counter.

The sergeant didn't lift his nose from the document. It was as if he hadn't noticed her enter. People often overlooked her, but she had expected better here. She waited. No response. She cleared her throat. He didn't budge. A cardinal error that many make is to assume that old people aren't in a hurry. How wrong can they be? When you've got a lot fewer years ahead of you than you've already used up, every little thing assumes greater urgency. When you've not got much of something it's advisable not to waste it. She reached into her handbag.

"My husband's dead and I don't know what to do with this."

She thrust the gun into the space between face and paper as she spoke.

In a matter of moments, the desk sergeant was transported from the concentration of his bureaucratic world, through the disturbing existence of violent crime and on to the afterlife. His heart, abused by years of sedentary policing and several hundredweight of canteen pastries, couldn't cope with the shock of being threatened out of the blue with a firearm.

The noise of his bulk striking first the counter then the floor brought a young PCSO running to the front desk. He stared at Sergeant Jenkins. He stared at the old woman with the gun. He put his hands up.

"D-d-don't d-d-do anything r-r-rash."

What a stupid thing to say to a crazy woman who clearly had already done the rashest of rash things.

'Anything else r-r-rash."

"My husband's dead. Is the sergeant also?"

PCSO Wallis wouldn't have known a dead body if he tripped over one, something he had almost done very recently. "I think so. Shall I call an ambulance?"

"If he's dead, you'd better make it one of those private ones. You know, they look a little like plumber's vans, but with blacked out windows and without the sign saying nothing of value is left inside overnight. I suggest, young man, that you think carefully about your next move."

Wallis's initial impression of the gun-toting pensioner were confirmed. She had just killed two men, maybe more, and, calm as you like, she was warning him that he was at risk of following them.

"Are you ready to take this?"

Her arm was beginning to ache and, as the gun shook in her hand, it seemed to follow with unerring accuracy the careful steps that PCSO Wallis was trying to make towards the door.

He misunderstood her meaning, shut his eyes, crossed himself and fainted.

She peered over the counter. Wallis was slumped across Jenkins's corpulent form. Unlike his superior, the younger officer would probably survive the shock, but it didn't look good, bodies piling up like that.

She wondered whether to wait for another officer to arrive on the scene. She could foresee further misinterpretation, maybe more casualties. On balance, placing the gun on the counter and leaving seemed the most sensible option. The initial wisdom in her autosuggestion was trumped by the concern that a villain might find it before the police did.

She slipped the weapon back into her bag.

As she fought to pull the door open, she didn't notice the security camera high up or the bright yellow notice beneath it. 'NOT IN USE OWING TO FUNDING CUTS'.

How the Other Half Lives

Knowing that a healthy body makes for a healthy mind, I get to the gym whenever I can afford it. And when I can't, I exercise by walking along the sea front. The other week one of my promenades took me to the harbour, where I saw a man hard at work cleaning a sleek cruiser.

"No slacking, there," I called out to him in my poshest voice. "I need it finished by the end of the afternoon."

"Is that your boat?"

I swung around to see a little old lady pointing at the vessel. What could I say, but "Yes, my love, that's one of mine"?

"I expect it cost you a lot of money."

"To be honest, I can't quite remember. A million and a half maybe. Something like that. All set against tax, of course."

"Of course," she echoed.

There was an uncomfortable pause before she asked if she could look around 'my' boat.

"Be my guest. Just take care on the jetty."

"That's very kind of you."

"Excuse me," I called over to the deck hand. "This young lady has permission to come aboard."

I wondered about scarpering while she took the tour, but that wouldn't have been very honourable, so I waited for her to return.

"Thank you, dear. That was marvellous," she beamed. "The master bedroom was particularly nice, but I don't see why you'd need a mirror on the ceiling."

I choked back a laugh, made my excuses and left.

Changing the World

Among the many drawbacks to sleeping rough in a shelter, the food waste left by its daytime inhabitants is perhaps the worst. Long after people have departed, the debris from their sandwich munching and crisp crunching acts as a beacon to rats. Not the sweet little ones in pet shops or medical labs; nasty Stephen King-sized ones.

I live my life wishing no harm on any living creature, but that doesn't prevent me from detesting these ravenous rodents. As soon as I discovered that I was sharing my nocturnal home with them, I knew I had three options. One, move somewhere else. Hardly an option, as safe places to sleep rough are in shorter supply than affordable housing. Two, try to ignore the rats. If you've ever found yourself in my situation, you'll know that's not viable. Three, find a way of getting rid of the rats. I chose option three. What choice did I really have?

Given my lack of funds and, of course, my principles, I realised I couldn't poison the vermin. I had to come up with a more intelligent, more humane solution. So, I invested in a couple of cans of dog food. What's that? No, I'm not barking mad. On the contrary, I figured that if I could lure some of the neighbourhood foxes to my shelter, they'd see off my unwelcome guests.

If you'll excuse the pun, I had to be canny, setting a small amount of the food some distance from my shelter in all directions, then gradually reducing the distance between my home and the bait. Within a matter of days, the foxes had grown accustomed to my presence. If you play it right, in time they take you for another fox. They know you're safe.

Before long, my foxy family had seen off the rodents. I guess the rats had two options, move somewhere else or get used to being eaten by the foxes. Hobson's Choice strikes again.

When it comes to foxes, familiarity breeds familiarity. I can identify all the individuals in the local skulk. The dominant male is, as far as I'm aware, the only tod in town with a complete brush, while one of the vixens has a damaged mouth, probably as a result of cutting herself on a discarded tin. Not one of mine, I hasten to add! Responding to a trail of crumbs that I laid out for her she has recently started to accept food from my hand. It's weird, feeling the teeth of a wild animal with a ferocious bite touching your skin, while remaining completely certain that you will not be bitten.

Who Am I ?

Iceberg

I'm an iceberg.
What you see ain't all you get.
What *do* you see?
A tramp or a dosser?
A dirty old tosser?
One of those ne'er do wells?
The source of bad smells?

Beneath the surface,
In the depths,
Away from which you steer
Your titanically important lives,
Lurks the rest of me,
The best of me,
The real me, if you like,
Whether you like it or not.

The loving mother,
The father seeking custody,
The accomplished chess player,
The published musician,
The soldier who defended your land,
The eco warrior,
The woman who shares what little she's got with
The guy who has less than that.

Captive Creativity

Humans are social animals. We depend on each other. You could say that being part of a group helps us survive ... and thrive. When we come into the world the first thing we have to establish is that we belong. That need to know that you belong repeats itself in every new situation.

When I received my first prison sentence, I had a good sense of where I belonged. No, not just with other criminals, but, more specifically, with other musicians. I was brought up by a bunch of hippies and from an early age my passion was music. By the time I learned to play the guitar, I had already had years playing with one.

On arrival in clink, I immediately tracked down my fellow music-makers. I quickly latched onto a drummer and a keyboard player, who shared with me the first rule of musical incarceration: volunteer for the chapel band. Religion wasn't my thing then any more than it is now, but I decided not to argue. For one these dudes were much bigger than me. Second, their advice offered me an unexpected chance to sustain my passion.

And so it came to pass that I gained access to a guitar. Nothing special, but x per cent of something is better than zero per cent of everything. And in return for playing at church services, I got to jam with my new mates during exercise breaks. The three of us really gelled and before long we'd put together an album or two's worth of original songs. Quite a mixture, some blues, some reggae, some rock.

Although the Governor was impressed by our devotion to duty on Sunday, he turned down our request to have a recording studio built. Of course, it was a crazy idea, but you get nowhere if you don't ask. Undeterred, we made a commitment to meet up when we'd completed our stretches and cut a disc. Leroy and I were released at about the same time, but Carl had another year to go. We weren't into letter writing but kept in touch with him via one of his girlfriends, who visited him from time to time. Most importantly, Leroy and I didn't tinker with what the three of us had produced inside. It wouldn't be right to take the project forward without Carl. Honour among musicians.

By the time Carl got out, I had scraped together enough dosh to book a day's recording with a sound engineer I half knew. Mate's rates. Everything was set. Like excited kids, Leroy and I were waiting outside a good hour before Billy, the sound guy, arrived to open up. We knew Carl would be late, he always was, so we weren't worried when the first hour passed without him. We made good use of the time, helping Billy get things balanced. Ten thirty, still no sign of our keyboard player, we started to get twitchy.

"Any off-licences between the station and here, Billy?"

"A couple, why?"

"Shit."

"You don't think he's …?"

"… that's exactly what I think. The bastard's getting pissed in a park."

We tracked Carl down shortly after eleven. He wasn't off his head and thanks to an all-day breakfast and three cups of coffee we were able to sober him up enough to get back to the studio for the remainder of the day.

Our anger with Carl for almost screwing everything soon gave way to the pleasure of being reunited as a band. The smiles didn't last long. Within a matter of bars, it was clear that Carl's soul - the thing he boasted of having tons of – wasn't in it.

"What the fuck's wrong, man?" Leroy growled. "Rick's forked out a fortune for this place and that's how you repay him?"

You don't mess with Carl. Not only is he a big bugger, but he's aggressive with it. That's the combination that keeps getting him sent down, his temper and his fists. Leroy was taking a bit of a risk laying into him, even though what he said was true. I could see Billy getting twitchy behind the glass.

But Carl didn't smash Leroy up or trash the studio. He simply pushed his stool back from the keyboard and hung his head. Looked as if he was going to cry.

"Are you all right mate?"

"No, Rick, I ain't. I've lost my mojo."

"The great Carl Simmonds losing his mojo? You're kidding."

"It's true. When we were all banged up, the music just flowed through me and from me."

"It still can."

"Don't think so. Inside music was my liberation. Being locked up seemed to release my creative juices. Now I'm out, they've stopped flowing. Like they've got no reason to exist, nowhere to go."

Somehow, we coaxed him into doing a few sets, but to be honest, we were just stumbling through the rest of the session.

Standing outside the studio, I made some bullshit excuse for not going to the pub with them, but we parted on good enough terms.

"No hard feelings, Rick?"

"No, Carl."

"See you around then?"

"Probably when we're next sent down."

The big man laughed.

We went our separate ways.

As I headed off to the latest in a long line of temporary accommodation, I recalled another example of 'Carl's Crisis', Richard Lovelace's seventeenth century poem from prison to Althea.

> *Stone walls doe not a prison make,*
> *Nor iron bars a cage;*
> *Minds innocent and quiet take*
> *That for an hermitage;*
> *If I have freedom in my love,*
> *And in my soul am free,*
> *Angels alone that soar above*
> *Enjoy such liberty.*

Standing My Ground

A scene from a Clint Eastwood movie, the Man With No Name opposite a bunch of mean hombres, at least ten of them. Only this time the fifty or so yards between them was not an arid prairie but the lush green of my local park. No horses. A man and a dog, my faithful Brutus. Me against a dirty dozen. Straight up, twelve against one. If I make it to old age, my grandchildren may hear that the gang was forty of fifty strong, but right now there's no need to exaggerate.

What possessed me to take on these crazy sods at crazy odds? It's a long story and all you need to know is that I'd been having a little local difficulty with this bloke, a dispute over scrap metal that developed into his car getting damaged. Then the threats, non-stop texts and voice mail messages warning what was going to happen to me. That's what really did it, him and his mates trying to mess with my mind. I don't like spending my time looking over my shoulder. That's how people bump into lamp posts. So, I decided to call him out. Meet in a secluded area of the park, where dog-walkers never go, early evening, before the doggers move in.

It was supposed to be just him and me settling the score, but for some reason he'd turned up mob handed. It was if he didn't trust me. That really riled me. My hunch was that the other eleven weren't there to spectate.

Decision time. Stand my ground or run?

I ran.

Towards the enemy.

Letting go of Brutus's lead, I took the baseball bat from inside my jacket and swung it around my head as I charged.

I can imagine what you're thinking. What a stupid thing to do. You'd be right, of course, though a little background might change your view.

As a kid I had just about everything awful that a kid can have. I don't mean measles and stuff like that. No, I copped all the psychological and neurological stuff: ADHD, ODD, attachment disorder, a touch of autism and … the list goes on.

I was on so many pills that I used to rattle. (The old ones are the best ones.) On my eighteenth birthday, I vowed I'd never again take a prescribed tablet. The net effect of all this was that I was vulnerable. I don't blame my mum, I understand why she was so protective, but it meant that I didn't have much resilience. To make matters worse, whenever something bad happened, I assumed it was my fault. For instance, when, aged ten or eleven, I was beaten up after school by three older kids, who I'd never seen before and haven't seen since, for something that they didn't mention and I couldn't remember doing, I simply accepted that I must have been in the wrong. Correction: when I said I had no resilience, in one respect that wasn't true. Whenever I've taken a beating, and there have been a few, I've always stayed on my feet. So, when the three teenagers had finished with battered, bruised and bloodied me, I was bent over double, hands on my knees, arse resting against a wall. And a smile on my face! I guess that, by the end of primary school, I'd realised that I could always have the last laugh, however bad things were.

Taking on a gang of twelve large, angry blokes is a good example of things being bad. But as I closed the gap, I could hardly believe my eyes. Mister Big's buddies were turning on their heels and legging it. Perhaps they didn't like baseball or were afraid of dogs. For whatever reason, in a flash it was just me and my arch opponent on the battlefield. I shouted to Brutus to sit. Yeah, I could've let him take a chunk out of the bloke's ankle, but I'm old-fashioned in my beliefs about fair fights. You might not think it was all that fair. My enemy towered over me like Goliath over David. Then again, we all know what happened in that one.

I think 'Grizzly' (what a pathetic nickname) was surprised by the mass desertion by his army and I took advantage of him momentarily being caught off guard by whacking him as hard as I could in the balls. It doesn't matter how big you are, your testicles are as sensitive as the next man's. As 'Grizzly' doubled over, I struck him on the back of his head and he fell to his knees like the proverbial bag of spuds. That was probably enough for him to know who he'd been picking on, but I put the boot and bat in a few times for good measure. You may think that this was violence beyond the call of duty, but I put it to you that if I let 'Grizzly' off lightly, he might perceive a weakness in me that he could exploit in the future.

As it was, he answered my question about being done in the affirmative. He even held his hand out from his prone, face-down position to shake on our deal.

If you knew my whole story, your hair would probably turn white. And there's a good chance you'd have a low opinion of me, over some of the things I've done. So be it. We can't agree on everything. But one thing I bet we do see eye to eye over is this: whoever you are, you must always stand your ground.

Justice

I know that other people cannot catch autism off me, but in my experience my condition has the worrying effect of eliminating their senses. Many people don't see me, at least, not for who I am, while others lose the power of hearing when they come into contact with me. For the record, one: I am *not* a label, two: I am entitled to be heard.

When I was little, I was told, like all kids are told, that the policeman was a friend, someone who could be trusted to help you. As I grew a bit older and a lot wiser, I came to understand that these reassuring messages were bullshit.

A few years ago, I had an urgent need of police assistance. My father was doing the most awful things to my mother. 'Abuse' doesn't begin to describe the way he treated her. I felt powerless to protect her or challenge him. Where could I turn if not to the wonderful police service.

I am not an idiot, but I felt one after my failed attempt to have a voice and, through my testimony, to give my mother a voice too.

I don't give up easily, but my persistence with the police

got me nowhere. Neither rank nor gender made any difference. To a man (and woman), the response was always the same:

They
blanked
patronised
doubted
humoured
ignored
disregarded
obstructed
belittled
And disbelieved me.

None of them said 'You haven't got anything important to say because you are a disabled nobody', but you don't always have to use particular words to get your message across. I see a parallel with the Stephen Lawrence case. The officers involved didn't make a statement to the effect that they wouldn't put themselves out too much because dead niggers didn't count, but a public enquiry found the Met to be institutionally racist. It doesn't matter if 'disablist' isn't a real word. It's how I was made to feel that counts.

Although I have good reason to resent the way in which the police have prevented me from having a voice, they're not the only ones who are meant to help but whose performance isn't what it says on the tin. Take social services (for a long walk off a short pier). They are beyond useless. I'll admit that I didn't persevere with them as much as I did with the law. While I lived in hope that there might be an officer who would take me seriously, in no time at all I realised that I couldn't take any social workers seriously.

Being asked to articulate my needs and told that it was 'up to you' was a bit like telling a blind man to find his way across widest section of the M25. (Yes, I know no-one is allowed to walk on a motorway, let alone across it!) I am on the autistic spectrum, and not just at the fluffy end, and that means that complex relationship stuff is 'a little' tricky for me to work out.

> What do you need
> Patronised
> Disabled
> Young Man?
> It's
> Up
> To
> You.
>
> I
> DON'T
> FUCKING
> KNOW!
> THAT'S
> WHAT
> I
> NEED
> HELP
> WITH!

And so, to school. There were times when it was OK, but the strongest memories are of how awful it was. Think about your own schooldays and there's a fair chance that some of the strongest recollections will be of the teachers you couldn't stand. In adult life, you'll probably have ended up steering clear of their subjects that turned to dust in their hands. Of course, after the first rush of bitterness, you'll remember the good guys too, those teachers who inspired you with their love of literature, or chemistry or woodwork, or whatever it is you have a life-long affection for. School is as much a place of injustice as the police station or social services offices.

I want to press the 'PAUSE' button. If I'm coming across as someone whose only paranoid message is how badly the world has treated him, I need to clarify. My hate of injustice isn't personal, it's global. My notion of what is just or unjust may not be the same as yours, but that's not my concern. Where I see something that I call injustice my blood boils. There was a time when boiling blood meant losing it, physically as well as emotionally. Nowadays, my response to injustices tends to be less explosive but, I hope, more effective. Based on thought out protest rather than gut reaction. If I can use a phrase that currently is in common use, I am a fan of justice for the many, not the few.

When my school introduced a new policy on mobile 'phones - they were not to be seen or heard – this bothered me a little, as my safety plan states that I must have mine handy at all times. What bothered me even more was that the policy wasn't being applied equally. It seemed that some kids were being rewarded for bad behaviour. You know the sort of thing, after a dozen refusals. "If you put your phone away, you'll get a treat'. Others, the ones that never messed around, seemed to be getting sanctions for the slightest breach of the rules. Faced with this inequality, I had no choice but to put the new regime to the test.

I took my 'phone out of my pocket and waved it in the air.
"Miss, I've got my 'phone out'. What are you going to do about it?"
"Put it back in your pocket."
"That's not going to happen. What will you do when I don't follow your instructions?"
"You know the rule."
"That's not the point."
"I think you'll find it is."
"I think you'll find me texting someone any minute now."
"Please put it away."
"Or giving someone a call."

"Please."
"Or surfing the net."
"What do you want me to do?"
"Follow the protocol."
"That's what I'm trying to do."
"I mean follow it fairly, firmly and consistently."
"You know where that could end up."
"Of course, I do. I'm not backing down."
"Please."
"I'll keep going until you have no choice but to exclude me."

I didn't go into school that morning planning to get excluded. But I have no regrets. How could I? I had taken a stand and exposed the nonsense of a rule. Having a few days to continue adapting our garden shed into a woodworking shop was an added bonus. Justice was served!

FTS

When you're applying for custody of your children, it doesn't help if your CV includes:

> Grim childhood, fucked up by the so-called 'care system'
> or
> Ten years as a heroin addict or
> Numerous convictions including for armed robbery or
> Numerous prison sentences or
> Not very complimentary psychological and psychiatric reports

With my life history including all the above, and then some, the custody hearings - the case took several months - were never going to be a doddle. I will tell you where I ended up, but I need you to show a little patience, while I flesh out some of the gory details.

From the age of 7 to 17, I was bounced around the care system, clocking up enough foster placements and children's homes to fill an 'I-Spy' book. I was abused. What do you expect? I was in the care system. Thankfully, it was never sexual, just physical. Mine isn't an ancient history, but it's only in recent years that the failings of parenting by the State has been fully exposed or that restraining kids by pinning them down or pressure against joints was outlawed.

As soon as I was old enough, I exploded out of the system like a champagne cork. I was free but rapidly discovered that freedom meant nowhere to go, no roof over my head, no food in my belly, nobody. Being in care wasn't a bed of roses; it was more like the shit you grow roses in. But when you're inside – yes, there are parallels with prison – at least you don't have the stress of not knowing where your next meal will come from or your next sleep will be. I've met loads of guys in prison who are so ill-equipped to cope with the world outside that the first thing they do on release is to assault a copper in order to be sent back down.

Ten years in care, then ten years of not caring ... about what I did, who I hurt, what risks I took, what rules I broke. As the song goes, 'I smoked a lot of dope and popped a lot of pills'. I became a narcotics mountaineer, starting at Base Camp Cannabis, then climbing up through Cocaine Pass, along LSD Ridge until reaching the twin peaks of Mount Heroin and Mount Crack. I became addicted because I didn't care. I didn't care because I was addicted. Symbiosis.

Addiction doesn't come cheap. Besides the psychological and physical costs, there's the wonga. I didn't maintain accounts during my decade of decadence, but I must have spent a six-figure sum feeding the monkey on my back. That was awkward, as I rarely had two pennies to rub together and none of the High Street banks were willing to lend me vast sums of money. So I did what any self-respecting addict would do. I begged and stole, but didn't borrow.

Never a lender or borrower be!

In true Hollywood style, the catalyst for change was the birth of my first son. It nearly wasn't, for while my partner was in the delivery room, I was a few paces down the corridor, smoking heroin in the toilet. Of all the things I'd done up to that point, I knew that now I'd reached rock bottom. From there, the only way was up and I was determined to get clean.

My relationship with rehabilitation services was very brief. I soon sussed that they had a vested interest in junkies staying addicted. How else do you explain why a lot of patients end up on increasing levels of methadone? And, as services get paid by the number of addicts they help, that's one hell of an incentive for getting *and keeping* as many people on the books as they can.

That left me with no other option than DIY detox. It was the hardest thing I've ever done. 'Cold turkey' doesn't begin to describe the process. It was more like being trapped on a giant poultry farm! But I knew this was the only way for me to get clean, really clean, squeaky clean.

My investment paid dividends, not only for me, but also for my son. My relationship with his mum held together and, after seven years, she gave birth to our second child. My balloon of joy was deflated more than a tad by the fact that, during pregnancy, my partner had been using. Discovering that my newborn son had been born an addict had a dramatic effect. The world went into free-fall, my partner and I fell out big time and she had the police remove me from our home, which had only one name on the tenancy agreement, and it wasn't mine. I left with nothing but the clothes I stood up in and a few quid in my pocket.

I was no stranger to tough times or rough sleeping, but coming after several positive years, this time it felt like being kicked repeatedly in the balls. I was down, not out, determined to bounce back, which I did, thanks in no small way to the help I got from an amazing guy who runs a project for homeless and vulnerable people. He came with me to every meeting with social services, the housing department and the benefits agencies.

And when I was ready to go to court for custody of my lovely boys, he was at my side again.

Given my previous experiences with officialdom, I should have been prepared for the absurd way in which every agency and service would respond to my case. However, in one respect I was forewarned and forearmed. For every interview and court appearance, I wore a long-sleeved shirt or jumper, concealing the one tattoo - I have a few - that might upset the powers that be. Three letters, 'F T S'. I'm sure you can work it out for yourself, but I'd rather not leave it to chance. *Fuck The System.* Offensive? I won't deny it. More offensive than the system, whether that means care, the courts, social services, housing or, most recently, the scandalous Universal Credit scheme, does to the most vulnerable in our society? I defy you to prove it.

My story doesn't have a happy ending. How can it? It hasn't ended yet and my current battle with UC-driven debt and pending homelessness is anything but rosy. However, I am the bringer of some good news. After months of battling, I did win custody. With the tide turning in my favour, my ex withdrew her opposition.

Although I didn't start telling these chapters of my story with a moral in mind, there is something vital to be learned from my experiences.

What matters most is
Who you are.
Not who you were.

Rowley

Moments before the end, the predator and the prey are indistinguishable in their stillness, both frozen, one by concentration, the other by fear. In that snapshot there is no telling whether the raccoon is poised to snatch a hen or hoping to avoid the cougar's bite. Does the cougar have the raccoon in its nostrils or the scent of the only creature it has to fear?

    Rowley presented the same confusion. I watched him, sitting with his forearm supported by the scarred Formica tabletop, his fingers wrapped around the coffee mug, long since cooled. He remained motionless, save for the subtle movement of his eyes. They were yellowed by age and hardship but had lost none of their sharpness. No expression, no clues as to his state of mind. I could invent and dispel multiple interpretations - furtive opportunist, weary victim, watchful philosopher - with equal uncertainty. So far as I could tell, Rowley didn't do anything. He just sat there in his woolly hat, which was far too small for his giant's head, pushed down so that his ears stuck out at right angle. His jumbled grey, white and black hair tumbled from beneath his hat, before coming to rest on his shoulders. Whatever the season, whatever the reason, he sported the same padded coat.

    In the absence of a reliable history - he had provided only the minimum required information to gain admission and even these sparse, written details were of questionable parentage - others were left to fabricate plausible, and implausible, accounts. To some he was a former member of the SAS or SBS, unable to manage the readjustment to civilian life. Although Rowley had none of the trademark tattoos, this was one of the more likely tales, given the number of ex-soldiers sleeping in shop doorways. A more colourful account had him as a double or triple agent in a previous incarnation, who remained capable of bringing down governments if ever he revealed the secrets between his ears. I avoided the more lurid and fanciful stories, preferring to see Rowley for what he was in the here and now, just another guy who had fallen into a dark hole with little obvious prospect of clambering back out. What we can't fathom about a person doesn't give us licence to fill the gaps with the first nonsense to come into our heads.

Don't get me wrong. He was an enigma. Take his name, Rowley. The unanimous verdict: a nickname, the same one as attributed to King Charles the Second, because it was alleged that his highness's sexual exploits matched those of his prize stallion, *Old Rowley*. Our Rowley didn't strike me as a latter day Cassanova but looks can be deceptive. One way or another, the rumour-mill cranked into action again. Our man's name indicated descent from the Stuart monarchy, an association with Newmarket racecourse's Rowley Mile, where he had lost a fortune, or a mystical and misspelt connection with the Rollright Stones in Oxfordshire.

I watched him for the best part of an hour. Apart from his shifting gaze, his only movements were the withdrawal of his gloved hand to surrender his coffee mug to Kathleen and the return of the same hand to the refreshed drink she brought him. Not so much as a murmur of thanks. There are two ways of playing things where Rowley and I found ourselves. You're thankful for small mercies, even though these cannot begin to compensate for the bigger picture, or as you have nothing for which to be grateful in that big picture, you see no value in thanking anyone for anything trivial. Up to that point, I didn't have Rowley down as an ingrate. Not that I'm in any position to judge. We all have valid reasons for the decisions we take and the moves we make.

As far as I know, Rowley didn't talk to anyone. No-one admitted to holding a conversation with him and, inevitably, this lack of communication spawned further theories. He was born dumb, was an elective mute following an early childhood trauma, his tongue had been cut out by Al-Qaeda or his voice box had been destroyed by narcotics. Take your pick, they were all as (un)likely as each other. I assumed that Rowley *had* spoken to the centre manager, who had the ability to draw even the most taciturn clients out of their shells, but nobody ever witnessed such an interaction.

Rowley's appearances at the Centre, although not regular, were never more than a few days apart. Speculation, which surrounded Rowley as thickly as the smoke that belched from his battered pipe, was at a premium during the interludes between his attendance. At the absurd end of the spectrum were rehashed versions of his career in the armed forces or intelligence service. More down to earth commentators focused on his likely whereabouts. In the absence of local sightings, it was assumed that he had found shelter further afield, under canvas, sofa surfing, or, back to craziness, at the country retreat of a wealthy dowager, whose life he had saved.

When we didn't see him for three weeks, we knew something was up. As usual, stories abounded: he had been summoned out of retirement for a top-secret mission in a distant land, received an unexpected inheritance from a distant relative or the afore-imagined dowager, gained employment on a cruise ship voyaging to distant ports. Only this time the fantasies lacked even a hint of conviction.

Family Matters

There was trouble aboard the Brighton bus. Rye had expected trouble sooner or later in her journey. She had put off going until loneliness and hopelessness drove her out.

She was finally going to visit her father who lived in the down- town area. It was not a very respectable area and she had put this visit off until the nights were lighter.

Nevertheless, two homeless guys had jumped on the bus as it waited for the lights to change. The driver was too late closing the doors and they squeezed in laughing uproariously. Once inside they proceeded to solicit money from all those onboard and flirt with the young women. Her stop came into view and she rang the bell. The boys insisted on escorting her off the bus in such a dramatic way that she laughed out loud.

Finding the apartment was not easy as signs on the buildings were damaged but she finally found Prospect House. Not having seen her father for such a long time she was apprehensive at meeting him now.

The climb to the fourth floor took time as the elevator was out of order but eventually, she stood, catching her breath, outside his door. This was it. Flat 20.

After ringing the bell nothing happened for a while until she became conscious of an eye observing her through the spy hole.

"Hello there. Can you open the door?"

A child's voice came back faintly "My dad told me not to open the door to anybody I didn't recognize. Who are you?"

"If your dad is William Rye, then I am your sister. I'm Valerie Rye" she said savouring the words "I think it is ok for you to talk to me."

Getting Custody

I had a reasonably happy childhood; my sister and I being raised by a single mum. However, she was violent towards me, always telling me I was like my dad, who was a bad lot. I ended up dealing drugs in Portsmouth for a number of years and was homeless for ten years.

Word of mouth brought me to the Mission, homeless and suffering severe depression. The welcoming atmosphere made me feel like a real person, with no judgements made.

I came to Eastbourne to be near my son. My ex only allowed "off -and on" access to him which almost tipped me over the edge. Childrens Services gave me access to him as she was on drugs. That motivated me to stop feeling sorry for myself and I spent ten months proving myself to the courts and ended up with full custody of my son, seven years ago. Being with him gave me a sense of purpose, helped me to keep busy and took my mind off other things going on in my life.

We have made a more normal life for ourselves that we enjoy.

I am thankful for my son but haven't seen my mum for ten years, since she was violent with him when she took him on holiday with her.

I began to volunteer at the Mission while I was still on the street, as I began to see my way a bit clearer. They say, "crime is common, logic is rare" and this is true in my case, my thinking was not always logical for a long time.

Because of my own life and family history, I can understand how others feel and know how to help those who come to the Mission. I can appreciate their frustrations with officials and can help in coping with the long telephone waits needed to speak to people at the Council and Social Services.

I still sometimes feel worthless, but it is getting better.

Real or Fantasy?

"Hi Jack. You are looking very smart."

"I've just had my hair and beard cut, so am feeling really good."

"That is good news. It makes you look younger."

"Come on, we have known each other long enough for you not to tell me untruths" he grinned, his expression belying his words. I had obviously made him feel even better.

As I looked at him, I thought how far he had come, even if he still had bad days. Most of the time he was able to look after himself and eat regularly. This was much better than a year ago when he had been just skin and bone and walked around in a daze when he happened to be sober.

"I hate to change the mood of the conversation but, have you heard that Carole died?"

"Oh, no? When?"

"About three weeks ago. It was cancer."

"Wow. What a shock. I think you two lived together at one time, didn't you?"

"We did, but I couldn't cope with all her phobias. It made

ordinary life very difficult and even affected going shopping for food."

"I remember her as a lovely lady, always smiling and interested in other people, but of course, I didn't live with her."

We went on to share our memories of Carole, both good and bad. I remembered that when she was off her meds, she couldn't keep her hands still, that they shook all the time. That made it difficult to hold cups and deliver them full to the guests who had requested them. She was very angry when Freddie suggested that it might be better to help in the shop, rather than serve food and drink in the Drop-in Centre. Helping in our charity shop worked out for a while until she began to harangue customers about their lives and faith.

Jack shared good times with Carole and her son when he was young.

"I remember that his favourite story was Peter Pan. He loved all the flying around and the appearances of Tinkerbell. He was convinced that one day he would be able to fly himself."

We chuckled and shook our heads at the gullibility of children as John finished up his bangers and mash and started on the jam sponge and custard.

"When the crocodile bit off Captain Hook's hand, Pete was very upset and started to have nightmares so often that we stopped reading the book. He would wake up in the middle of the night screaming, "I can't feel my hand. Where has it gone?"

It was a long time before this stopped and even as he grew older, he would stop whatever he was doing, from time to time and peel off his left glove to check that all his fingers were present on that hand."

As Jack reminisced about those times with Carole and her son and events that had happened more recently, he smiled wistfully "I suppose it's like the ticking crocodile, isn't it? Time is chasing after all of us."

Waiting

Where was he? He was usually in every day for breakfast and then went off to his pitch outside the Coop on Terminus Road. What had happened? We began to think he might have been moved on by the police or had even spent a few nights as a guest at the local nick.

He was a tough old bird and had been a soldier in his youth, serving in the Falklands. This had gained him a service pension and a slight limp. Leaving the service was followed by unemployment and eventually homelessness. After all what job did yomping across South Georgia fit you for? And how could you cope with not having someone else to tell you what to do and when and how to do it? He now rented a room in a shared house down the road. Then, two weeks later, he limped in, looking a bit worse for wear. What had happened? The bloodshot eye could have been caused by a fall or "walking into a door." The real reason was he had been attacked by a gang of youths and taken by ambulance to the Conquest Hospital where he was admitted to the Neuro Ward with bleeding on the brain.

A few days later, he came back, accompanied by his son. This tall, tanned man was a forestry manager in North Yorkshire and, being out of touch with his dad had only just heard what had happened. Driving through the night, he looked tired and frustrated by his father's obvious need for help, yet unwillingness to ask for it. The son grinned as he explained "I like to make use of what I know, but in this situation, I am totally out of my depth, so we need your help?"

Sitting down with him, we discussed Bob's situation. He was already in receipt of Pension Credit, having reached retirement age a few months before. If these injuries were permanent, they would add to his disability. Was he eligible for an Attendance Allowance? His son was concerned that his dad couldn't manage on his own, now being very much more unsteady on his feet and often quite confused. He explained that he could only stay for the next month but then must go back to his work in Settle.

Sitting down in the Mission with mugs of tea and plates of sausage casserole and mash they waited as Maria tried to get in touch with Adult Social Care. Knowing that these things invariably took a lot of time, she prepared them for a long wait. This long wait was repeated each day over the next three days until finally they were able to speak to someone.

A smiling pair pushed the door open and sat down at the admin desk and reported good news. Someone from Adult Social Care had phoned and they were coming to do a home assessment. All would now be well, wouldn't it?

Well, it would depend on what they found and how long the queue was for attention, but at least someone was coming, and they had promised him a place in a local Day Care Centre.

My Daughter

I moved from Cornwall to Eastbourne to be closer to my daughter in January 2022, with the promise of a job and accommodation, which didn't materialize. I became homeless and slept on the beach.

I was at the end of my tether and with only 6% charge left on my phone, I Googled "homeless shelters" in Eastbourne and up came M25M.

Key Workers there referred me to the Council who wouldn't accept duty of care for me and tried to send me back to the West Country. Apparently, a child does not count as a connection with the town. I must have walked twenty miles a day looking for work and after that accommodation. Eventually I did find somewhere to live and now I have part time work as a carpenter.

Back in Cornwall we had been about to buy a house together when my partner found out she was pregnant. While I was working away from home to get money to purchase the house, she moved back to Eastbourne where her family lived and tried to cut me out of the child's life.

In order to be able to meet up with my daughter I spent a lot of time and money at the Family Contact Centre and this persistence paid off. I now have access to my daughter who is four years old.

Now life is amazing. I volunteer at M25M to give back some of what was given to me. I am a devoted dad who moved hundreds of miles to be near his daughter and am working on improving the relationship with my ex.

Getting There

Jim is an ex- guardsman, who did two tours in Northern Ireland during "The Troubles, as well as guard duty at Buckingham Palace and Windsor Castle. He joined the army because he got his girlfriend pregnant and wanted to provide security for her and the baby.

His tour in Northern Island was difficult and dangerous and he had to concentrate on his duties there rather than worry about his girlfriend.

On returning from Northern Island, he went to find out how they were, but she decided she didn't want him and denied him access to the child. "I never had the chance to be a father."

After leaving the army, he did bar work and eventually became homeless. Contact with the Mission was through an ex-partner who volunteered there. He still has bad weeks and days, but now, life is becoming better. There are days at a time when he knows where he is and what is the date. He still can't always remember appointments and needs someone else to remind him, the day before.

Ordinary, everyday things now come into focus, and he knows where to shop for food and when to change his bed. He now has a dentist and is now getting his eyes sorted out. Everything is coming together.

Below are his thoughts about M25M -
They don't judge people. If you need help you can get it.

The sound of voices, knowing that other people are around.
A nice place to come when you've got nowhere.
Everybody here has got different things going on. You don't need to get involved; you can just be there.
This place has probably saved my life a few times when I have been down.
Places like this help you see others who are worse off than you.

Going Down the Road

"I have nothing in the cupboard" I thought as my stomach gurgled and complained. I knew that there was a place down the road where they gave out Food Bank vouchers. No, I couldn't cope with people asking too many questions about my life. I decided not to bother.

However, two days later, having run out of coffee and sugar, I could not go on. I would have to swallow my pride and go down the road. Life had become more and more difficult as I felt more and more ill. No point in going to the doctor, he would shake his head and tell me to go home to Yorkshire.

He did have a point; my daughter and her husband had offered me a home with them, and their children and my sister had offered her spare room. The thought of driving three hundred miles was just too much, even if I could scrape together enough money for the petrol. There was nothing for it; I would have to go down the road.

Gathering all my strength and courage I walked up the steps and pushed the door open.

"Hullo, love. How are you doing?"

I mumbled something about not being too bad and managed to stutter "I need a Food Bank voucher."

"Sit down, have a cup of tea and let's see if we can sort it out."

After two cups of tea, spaghetti bolognaise and some ice cream I was feeling much better, especially as I had the voucher tucked safely in my purse.

Going down the road became a regular event for a cup of tea and a chat with the people who sat at the different tables, some eating and drinking, some drying off from the rain, some catching up on the sleep they had not managed in their tent up on the Downs. Talking with one of the Key Workers I realized I might be entitled to a disabled badge for my battered old car and even more wonderful, I could apply for a Personal Independence Payment (PIPP) because of my mobility problems.

We sat down to fill in the appropriate application forms, but it all took a lot longer than I expected. The forms were so complicated. Thank God for Maria's help.

As I began to eat more regularly and socialize with other people at the Centre, I began to feel much better in myself. I knew that, now, I could manage in my first floor, bed-sit, however, I dreaded the future. How would I manage if I got ill again and how would I cope as I got older?

Maybe it was time to go home. I had been away far too long, and I had almost forgotten the reasons why I had left. I had enough credit and charge on my mobile phone and before I knew it, I was dialing my sister's number.

"I am so glad that you called. When are you coming home?"

At this, I burst into tears. She wanted to see me despite all that had happened. After I had dried my tears and my voice settled down, I found myself agreeing to travel north as soon as I had enough money for the petrol. I had very little to pack so there was nothing to keep me in Eastbourne. Except one thing. I needed to go down the road.

Walking into the Centre felt like coming home and a small part of me began to regret leaving. I smiled to see my friend on duty. Putting a box of chocolates on the table, I managed to find the words to thank her for her help and warmth. Giving her the good news about my disabled badge and PIPP I explained that I would no longer be coming down the road to see her as I was going home at last.

Misery

Back in the days when everyone was old and stupid. I never felt like that, she thought to herself. In those days she was ambitious, attractive, and wanted.

She looked back at that time with nostalgia. It had been good to be alive. Life had been fun. She had aimed high in those days, a scholarship to Oxford, drinking champagne cocktails with all the bright young things who eventually became boring, middle-aged politicians.

When had she realized that nobody really cared about her? Shortly after graduation she discovered she was pregnant and the one she suspected was the father, refused to have anything to do with her or even pay for an abortion. She went home to her parents in their council house in Luton expecting that they would help. No such thing. Her father washed his hands of her and threw her out of the house. Forced to sleep on her cousin's sofa she tried to think out what to do. Eventually the cousin needed his sofa, and she was out on the street.

You might have expected the street homeless community would look after her. They usually did so for waifs and strays like her, but not this time. They found her high and mighty attitude irritating and made an excuse to get rid of her by reporting her to the police for a robbery she had not committed. This was her one piece of luck. In prison she was looked after and when her baby was born in the prison infirmary, she looked forward to starting a new life.

However, this was not to be. Deemed incapable of looking after a child, she had to say goodbye to her son after six weeks when he went to be fostered. She was on her own again. Things went from bad to worse and the only way she could survive was to go "on the game". She hated the fat, sweaty bodies and shuddered every time someone touched her. I can't take any more of this, she thought as she stood on the bridge and looked down at the black water beneath. Maybe this was the only way to find peace. No one would miss her or mourn her death. She climbed on to the wall and prepared to jump...

Elsie

It came like magic in a pint bottle: it was not ecstasy but it was comfort. Winds howling around and through the flimsy cardboard that Elsie called home made her clutch her bottle close to her chest weakened by too many months spent out in the elements.

Sips from her bottle kept Elsie going. She knew from her days in the other world she'd inhabited, that the warmth she felt as the liquid slid over her tongue and down into the depths of her throat and beyond, was not real. It was a false warmth but it was as good as she had come to expect in the scarce life that embodied her.

In her younger days, Elsie was quite a stunner. Never short of male attention she'd led quite a glamorous life being taken to fancy restaurants, nightclubs and holidays. Her slender frame was a designer's gift as clothes hung beautifully on her. Even today, Elsie's figure was often envied by others who saw her without a grubby blanket wrapped around her. Somewhere through the years, Elsie lost her way. The love of her life turned out to be a narcissist, only interested in himself. Her children took after their father and much as she tried to bring them up to consider others, they too were confirmed narcissists, so full of their own importance, even now, they are not aware that their dear mother has only some cardboard to protect her from the rain, cold winds and gales when she sleeps. A far cry from the plush home they'd grown up in.

Elsie felt so beaten down by the time she was abandoned by her husband and children she couldn't summon the energy to fight for herself. Instead, she slid down the slippery slope that once on, is so difficult to escape from. Her initial horror of finding herself on the streets soon turned to gratefulness for the understanding the street community gave her as it welcomed her into its world.

Like so many before her, Elsie soon found solice and comfort in her bottle. If nothing else, she'd learned to hold onto her bottle, hold it tight to her soul, for if she dropped it, she'd have to endure the reality of her street world in all its horrific glory. She knew when it came like magic in a pint bottle, it was not ecstasy but it was comfort and that's what Elsie needed to get her through each day.

Volunteer Perspectives

Why do I Volunteer?

- I have always done charity work with Poppies and cancer organisations. I have had it tough, and people have had to help me, so I want to give something back.

- I have known Oscar for many years and, after retirement and being widowed, was bored and getting depressed. I came in for coffee with Oscar who, knowing I had always wanted a van, offered that I could drive the Mission van during the week, picking up donations, and use it for my personal use at the weekends. I am told that now I am a different man.

- I used to regularly go into town on Saturday to shop with a friend. We began to see the same guy begging on the street and, on chatting to him, discovered he was the same age as our eldest sons. This pulled on our heart strings, and we got involved with the groups that provide food and drink around Bankers Corner in the evenings, via mobile kiosks. Being asked questions by our clients that we couldn't answer we contacted M25M, and as they say, the rest is history.

- I have been involved for fifteen years. I was helped myself and I just want to help others, that is it.

- Because there is a need to help people going through difficult times.

- Because of the help I received from the Mission and how supported and loved they made me feel. I wanted to do that for others. The Mission staff scooped up my whole family and I wouldn't have a family or a life without the Mission.

- My brother was a guest here, back in the day when the charity was called Oasis Christian Outreach, so I knew about the work done here. At the start of COVID I saw people lining up to collect take away food, some of them with their children. I live round the corner and never gave the place a second thought, until then. This is my parish, so I am giving back to my community. The Mission is a family, they do what they do with love and care for their fellow human beings. 90% of the guest appreciate what we are doing. I get more out of being a volunteer that I do out of my paid job.

- This is what Jesus would do. There but for the grace of God go I.

- My first visit to M25M was to help a friend who was working in the garden. I didn't have any thought of being part of the volunteer's team at that time. While gardening we were asked to help serve tea and coffees when they were short of volunteers. As the weeks passed, I got to know the guests I got more involved. I love chatting to the guests and I am a good listener. Because I was a hairdresser, I started cutting people's hair and began to participate in the pastoral side and prayer ministry of the Mission' s work. I love being part of the M25M team, helping with the amazing work and love they offer to the community. I like the diversity of what I do, being able to connect with the guests through listening and showing empathy to each individual. I have made many friends among the family of M25M and want to carry on is this role. It is a wonderful oasis in the middle of Eastbourne.

Create Your Own Saint

"What are you doing sitting there, mate?" asked the little fellow with the beard, "What do you think you idiot? I'm sitting in this doorway waiting for the bus to Timbuctoo". The little fellow smiled and sat down next to the man and offered him a drink from a flask of coffee. "Naw, thanks, mate! I'd rather have a shot of vodka."

The two men sat and talked together and began to laugh at each other's jokes. Steve said "Ain't you got a home to go to either?" the little fellow answered "Yes, I do but I had a row with the wife. She wants me to stop picking up drunks in the street. What do you think?" This caused both of them to burst into laughter again. When they could speak, Steve was given a business card with an address on and told, "If you are still around tomorrow, drop into this place and get something to eat". Steve turned up his nose and started to give the card back, "Too many do-gooders around in these places that want to preach at you and try to stop you drinking. I know I've been to places like this before."

"Up to you mate, but the food is good and it's free". "What's the catch? Will they want me to go to church and stuff?" Ignoring these words, Steve's new friend ambled off down the road saying, "I better go and make my peace with the missus."

A week later Steve found that he hadn't eaten for four days, and he started to feel faint. He put his hand in his pocket and pulled out the card he had been given. He decided that he would face the possibility of being preached at for the chance of a hot meal. The place was further away than he expected and by the time he got there he was dead on his feet.

As he entered the hall he was greeted with "Hallo darlin' have you come to eat?"

"No, you daft cow I've come to see the Queen" She just laughed at him and said "Sit you down and we'll get you something to eat"

After digging into the food, he was able to lift up his eyes and across the room he could see the little fellow he had met in the shop doorway a week ago. Now Steve could see that he was chubby and off-white in colour. He was deep in conversation with an old woman who wore an assortment of clothes in different colours muffled up to the eyes in an old army great coat. As their conversation ended and she got up to go, he hugged her. Then he saw Steve and said "Now then you old bugger. So, you decided to come after all". Steve grinned and was about to come out with a mouthful of expletives when a young woman with bright red hair and purple trousers said "Be careful what you say mate. We think he's the closest thing this town has to a saint."

Pumpkin Soup

It was harvest time again, that time of year that came round quickly once summer was over. Every year churches, schools and clubs would sometimes donate improbable items of food such as tinned mussels, pate, foi gras, petits fours and exotic cheeses to a Drop-in Centre for vulnerable folks who were lucky to see cheddar cheese and tinned pears in their lifetime.

This year there was a surfeit of pumpkins of all shapes and sizes, already beginning to go off. What were we going to do with them? In a moment of madness, I suggested "Maybe we can make pumpkin soup?" All eyes fixed on me, and I realized that they thought I know what I was talking about.

"What a good idea. Can you organize it?"

That is how it came about that three of us spent hours peeling and chopping pumpkins, adding seasoning, and heating up huge cauldrons of the stuff. Now, we called it "alimony", in its original sense of "nourishment", but we weren't sure what our poor guests would call it, or even if they would eat it.

"We can't tell them it's pumpkin soup. You know how they

are about food they haven't tasted before and are sure they won't like."

"We could put in some of those potatoes and carrots and call it vegetable soup. That would make it more acceptable."

"Let's hope so. All we need is some volunteer who doesn't think before they speak or thinks it's funny to tell the guests what they have eaten."

This prompted us to close the kitchen to all but the cooks in the know, make a big show of collecting potatoes and carrots and quickly sling pumpkin peel and seeds into the food rubbish bin outside. We even posted a guard on the bins so nobody could look inside. In the end, the soup went down a storm and some even came back for second helpings.

Being so successful made a rod for our backs as we gained a reputation of being ace soup makers. Whenever any large quantities of vegetable of whatever variety was donated it was assumed that we would make soup.

It was noted by many that the pumpkins, which had been on display on windowsills, had disappeared and we had to say that they were being stored safely for Bonfire Night.

We thought we had been found out when one of our older guests, who had been on the road for thirty years, said "By heck, that soup was great girls, but I reckon there was more than potatoes and carrots in it."

He winked at us, as he walked out into the dusk to a cold night's sleep, bundled up in a sleeping bag on the seafront "Don't worry, love. I will keep your secret."

The Matthew 25 Mission Prayer
written by Father Neil Chatfield

O God, open our eyes that we may see the need of others
Open our ears that we may hear their cries.
Open our hearts that we may feel their anguish and their joy.
Let us not be afraid to defend the oppressed, the poor, the powerless, because of the anger and might of the powerful
Show us where love and hope and faith are needed and help us to bring them to those places.
Open our eyes and ears, our hearts, and lives, so that we may, in these coming days, be able to do some work of justice and peace for You.
Amen

BOURNE TO WRITE

Bourne to Write is an online creative writing workshop led by the writer, broadcaster and arts critic Roddy Phillips. The weekly Zoom workshops take a student-centred approach to creative writing, offering a range of strategies to help new writers develop their talent and skills. Writers are encouraged to explore their creative writing potential through self-awareness and self-discovery. Bourne to Write regularly publishes the work of its writers online and on amazon.

    The Zoom workshops are suitable for aspiring writers of all levels and abilities and for anyone with a strong interest in reading and writing, who would like to deepen their understanding of the creative process. Bourne to Write regularly publishes its writers work online and in paperback and on amazon. For more information on how you can join one of our workshops log onto...

bournetowrite.co.uk

Voices from the Margins

Printed in Great Britain
by Amazon